Chasing the Lost Dream

June 3, 2022

Enjoy the journey.

Jed C. Hossack

Chasing the Lost Dream

By: Joei Carlton Hossack
JoeiCarlton@Hotmail.com

Skeena Press
PMB 9385, P.O. Box 2428
Pensacola, Florida 32513-2428

SkeenaPress@Hotmail.com

Published by: Skeena Press
                  PMB 9385, P.O. Box 2428
                  Pensacola, Florida 32513-2428
                  SkeenaPress@Hotmail.com

Copyright: Joei Carlton Hossack © October, 2006
                  www.joeicarlton.com

Edited: Joei Carlton Hossack
                  Marian Montague-Bassett

Cover Design: Brion Sausser
                  www.BookCoverDesigner.com

ISBN: 0-9657509-6-5

Library of Congress Control Number: 2006907172

Printed in the U.S.A.   10 9 8 7 6 5 4 3 2

By the same author:

For **Harry and Sandra** who were always there when I needed them.

For **Phil and Andrea** who welcomed me with open arms when I showed up on their doorstep.

For **Jean and Bill** whose prayers are with me on every adventure.

For **Marjorie and Don** who are watching over me from above.

For **Stephen and Michael** who made both my journeys through Turkey fascinating and fun (mostly).

For **Paul** who is always in my heart.

Chasing the Lost Dream

Digging In

Turkey in the Middle

Czeching Out

Chapter 1

I Want My Life Back

"You don't have to do this, you know," said my sister-in-law Sandra. "You have lots of friends over there. You can have someone in England sell it for you. You don't have to go back," she said, her eyebrows knitting into deep creases. "Do you really think Paul would want you to go through so much pain?" she asked.

"Sandra," I replied showing a little annoyance along with gut-wrenching sadness and overwhelming confusion, "what's going to happen to me that is worse than has already happened? I must sell the van and I want it to be mine before I do. It has to be only mine. I have to get my life back. I need my life in some kind of order. I can't stand the way I feel. I feel like I'm in limbo."

I wanted to scream at her for being scared for me. I wanted to scream at everyone who was telling me how I should feel, what I should or shouldn't do, where I should or shouldn't go. I wanted to scream at the world. I wanted to scream at myself because I was so scared and confused.

*   *   *   *

When I told my sister, Mona, about my plans to return to England and spend my summer on archaeological digs she was as concerned as Sandra.

"You really don't have to do this," she reminded me over the phone from her home in California.

3

Chasing the Lost Dream

"Mona," I replied, " I don't care if they hand me a shovel and tell me to dig down to the next twelve centuries. I just want to run someplace, to do something.....anything.

"That's the problem," she said, "they'll give you a teaspoon and tell you to dig down the twelve layers, then someone will come along with a teeny-tiny paintbrush and with one little flick of the wrist, blowing softly on the centimeter of dust that is covering ancient history, will claim the glory."

"Mona," I asked, ignoring the previous comment, "do your friends still ask about me? Do they ask how I'm doing?"

"Yes" she replied, "all the time. They never heard such a sad story. It is every traveler's greatest nightmare that something will happen on a vacation when you're so far from home, but to be alone in a campground....." her voice starting to quiver. "Yes, they still ask how you're doing."

"The first time someone asks how I'm doing and you say "not too well, she's really depressed," they'll wait about a month and ask again. The second time you say "she's not doing well," they might ask again. The third time they ask and if I'm still not doing well they will not only stop asking about me but they will avoid you like the plague because they don't want to know."

"I understand what you're saying," she replied, "but what's your point?"

"The next time your friends ask how I'm doing you tell them that your sister is on an archaeological dig in England, and check out their reaction. They will hound you for every tidbit of information. They will want to know every minute detail. I don't care if it is boring. I don't care if it is backbreaking work. I don't care where I have to drive to find it. This is something that Paul and I wanted and planned on doing together. Besides," I said as cheerily as I could muster, trying to be optimistic, "just think of how this is going to look on my resume of life."

4

Digging In

"I know you're right," Mona replied. "I love you, and since I can't talk you out of it, please be careful."

"I will, I promise. I love you too. I'll write you all the time so you won't have to worry about where I am or what's happening to me. You know that I have lots of friends over there and I will contact them so I won't spend too much time on my own.

*   *   *   *

It had been almost a year since my husband Paul had died and most of the time the pain was still overwhelming, almost crippling. He died so quickly. We had been traveling through Germany on our way to Denmark, camping in a small van that we had named the Puddle Jumper. We had been on and off the road for about two-and-a-half years and still loved every minute of our adventures. He went jogging, had a heart attack and died in a stranger's car, never even getting out of the campground. His life and mine were over in minutes.

How a person's life can go from riding high to the depths of despair, in one stopped heartbeat, will always remain a mystery to me.

I wanted my life back!

Chapter 2

A Mind in Turmoil

I had never been a terribly organized person but I knew that I had to take care of things in order. If I never saw the van again and someone sold it for me I felt in my heart that I would never get beyond wanting to see the van where Paul and I had spent our happiest years together. I would spend the rest of my life regretting not having handled things myself. I would regret not having found some small hidden treasure that belonged to the man I loved and had shared my life with for over twenty years.

I needed to sit alone in the van and feel him all around me. I needed to see the only home we had had for the last few years of our life together; the place where we had spent months at a time enjoying a life that most people only dreamed about and, whether they admitted it or not, had envied.

I needed to do this as much as I needed air to breathe and water to drink. The sooner the pain was faced the sooner I could live with it. "Indeed," I said to myself, "what could happen to me that would be worse than had already happened?"

On the day of his death, June 26th, 1992 the last line of my diary read "My life is gone." I don't remember when I wrote it. I don't even remember writing the words. I do know that to this day those four simple words are still true. Losing Paul left a void in my life the size of the Grand Canyon and my heart shattered into so many pieces that there would always be a piece missing. He was the joy and the fun in my life. He took so much of my life with him when he left. I wanted a little piece of it back.

Digging In

I had to return to England. I had to learn to drive the van. When Paul was alive, I had only driven it when he insisted that I at least try it or when we had a bet on something stupid or a card game and I had lost. There were any number of things that he would do if he lost the bet but me.....I had to drive the damn van. He always insisted upon it and I always dreaded it.

I knew I would have to sleep in the van like we had done for those too few fabulous years on the road. I would force myself to camp in it but only in places where I felt safe. I would cook my meals in it and hope that the weather would be nice enough to eat outside like we had done so often. At any opportunity I would go over every inch of it looking for a treasure or two behind the cushions, at the back of a cupboard or under the seats. I would make it mine and then, and only then, could I let it go for someone else to love.

My family and friends felt it was too early and would be much too painful. I knew they were right. I had to do it anyway. How could I let the home we had traveled in for two-and-a-half years rust away with no care? That was unthinkable. We had loved our little home on wheels. We had loved the traveling.

We had loved being together even after sixteen years of marriage!

Chapter 3

Departure Day

Departure day was the pits. I got up before dawn, the knot in my stomach producing an incredible amount of heartburn, not letting me sleep any longer. I tried not to wake my brother and sister-in-law because it was much too early even for me, and since Paul's death I had become an extremely early riser.

I fumbled for the light switch in the living room, where I slept on a hide-a-bed, and then again in the kitchen. Despite the fact that kitchen switches are all in the same spot on the wall my fingers couldn't connect with this one until I slid my hand across the rough surface and made contact. I was still so tired that the bright overhead light produced sparkles and I had to blink a couple of times and focus before they went away.

I made a pot of coffee only after I opened and closed every cupboard to find the coffee and the sugar. The sugar bowl was filled with pink and yellow packets of various substitutes so I dipped my teaspoon into the five-pound bag of the real stuff and put two heaping spoonfuls into the biggest mug I could find. When it still wasn't sweet enough I emptied one of the pink packets into my coffee and headed back to my bed. I didn't last long sitting there with several pillows propping up my back, sipping my coffee and thumbing through a fashion magazine filled with advertisements for new lipsticks and hair shapes and colors.

I heard the thump, as the early edition of the newspaper hit the door. I opened it just wide enough to retrieve the paper. I was halfway through my first cup, the Toronto Star spread out over most of the kitchen table, when Harry, second oldest of my

Digging In

siblings, and Sandra, his partner of many years and a former schoolmate of mine, sauntered into the kitchen.

The coffee was okay for me but much too strong for them. They drank anyway, adding a few dribbles of hot water from the tap. We all sat like zombies staring into the blackness of our cups before actually figuring out who would be taking their shower first.

Harry went first and I followed. Sandra would wait until later in the day since she was the only one not traveling anywhere.

With pad and pencil I started making a list of the stuff I didn't want to forget. I poured another cup of coffee and could feel my brain slowly unfurling like a flag without benefit of a breeze, and reluctantly coming to life.

I carried the second cup around the living room with me. I made a little pile with my passport, plane ticket, some Canadian and American cash and traveler's checks, along with my little 'under-the-clothing' zippered pouch to carry my valuables safely. I made another little pile with a blank eight-by-eleven triple-sized notebook, several pens and a couple of pencils, an eraser and what I always refer to as my five-cent pencil sharpener, even though it cost me more than a dollar fifty. I was also trying to figure out what I needed in the way of clothes and minor incidentals to take with me, and to make a list of things to pick up while still in Canada.

Harry, Sandra and I had breakfast together before I kissed Harry goodbye and he left for the three-hundred-mile drive back to Montreal to visit his children, a ritual that he followed every three weeks.

I spent most of the day with Sandra and was very grateful for her company. We had talked in the morning and even though I hadn't said much about it, she knew I was scared

Chasing the Lost Dream

out of my wits. In the afternoon I packed all the little piles of stuff that were spread out all over the living room.

There were moments of relative calm mixed with frantic running around the apartment. I had been staying with them since returning from Florida where I had spent the winter.....the first winter on my own. I knew we were all happy that my visit would soon be over but that didn't make it any easier. Three adults in a one-bedroom apartment had not been an ideal situation, but somehow we had managed not to kill each other for the few weeks that I had invaded.

There were a few last minute telephone calls to friends to bid them a fond farewell and then a short drive to my nephew's house mid-afternoon to store my red Mazda pickup truck in his garage. Stephen got home shortly after I arrived. He had left work a little early so I wouldn't be late or anxious. We didn't sit around long.

Stephen, the older son of my brother Nathan, and I had a relaxing steak dinner at The Keg, one of the better chain-style restaurants. We talked little about my trip and I was grateful for that but I can't remember what we did talk about. I really couldn't concentrate.

Right after dinner, without lingering over coffee, we were off to the airport just a few miles away. We hugged and kissed on both cheeks at curbside in the "drop-off passenger" lane and I waved as he pulled away but I don't think he saw me.

After checking in and going through the metal detector and security I didn't have long to wait. There was just enough time to pick up a variety of hard candies, a chocolate bar and an interesting-looking novel. With the rest of the passengers I packed onto Air Transat flight number 258 and found my aisle seat.

*   *   *   *

Digging In

On a scale of one to ten, this plane trip was a minus forty. I had barely gotten comfortable, if that's possible in any seat other than first class, when the stewardess fumbled and spilled half of a can of caramel-colored soft drink down the sleeve of my brand new fuchsia-colored silk shirt. I washed it out immediately and it clung to me like some bratty little kid hugging his mother's leg for dear life not wanting to get into the dentist's chair. With stretching out the sleeve and fanning it with a magazine for the first half of the trip, it eventually dried with only a dark stain to show where the wet and sticky had been.

When I finally managed to fall into a groggy stupor, somewhere between sleep and wishing for the plane to crash and put me out of my misery, a stewardess, I sincerely hope not the same one, ran into my knee with the beverage cart. I awoke with a howl to discover that my seat mate, not someone I would have been the least bit interested in had he been the last man on earth, had his head resting on my shoulder. He was snoring loudly, and with an occasional snort thrown in for good measure, I found him to be totally disgusting. I was now in a really foul mood and shoved him aside with the grace and gentleness of a Sumo wrestler. I heard a couple of bones make a soft crackling noise as his head flopped to the other side. He never woke up and with the neck noises I had caused I wondered if he ever would!

I was a nano-second away from falling asleep again when a baby started crying. My first reaction was a loud groan and an under-my-breath mutter, "I'm getting too old for this crap," but, except for the baby and the baby's mother who couldn't have cared less, there was no one awake to hear me.

I know that I slept for some part of what was left of the night but I was up bright and early and had to squint as we aimed into the sun. Coffee was offered and gratefully accepted.

Chasing the Lost Dream

I was on my refill cup when the cart came by with the Styrofoam package that hid my breakfast tray. Despite my long, dreary night with little sleep, I was ravenous and although airplane food has little resemblance to real food I ate the soggy bacon and overdone scrambled eggs with gusto. By the time breakfast was over I was well fortified with caffeine. I would definitely make it through the day.

We landed at Gatwick at ten-thirty in the morning.

Chapter 4

Familiar Territory

I had landed at London's Gatwick Airport several times before but never under these confusing circumstances. I had always been with my husband who instantly knew where to go, how to get there and what to do when we arrived. Even if he was wrong, he was always a man of action and I always trusted him.

It took several minutes to get my bearings and I kept going over the instructions, hoping my instincts were right. I found my way to the shuttle bus that took me to downtown London. I was getting excited and nervous. I was about to make my way through the London transportation system alone for the first time. Once I got off the bus and into the underground subway system it didn't take long to find out which way to go. Unlike my husband I was not shy about asking for directions. I arrived safely with my luggage in tow at Victoria Station.

On one of the giant overhead information boards I found the listing for the train going to Otford-and-beyond along with the platform number. Since it was no longer rush hour I had over an hour to kill before boarding. I strolled around the station checking out the racks of mostly unfamiliar magazines. I drifted onto a couple of other platforms just to watch the trains coming in and going out. I checked on the exchange rate for the Canadian dollar against the British pound and ended my wanderings at the ladies' washroom. I pulled a handful of coins out of my pocket to see if I had ten pence for the pay toilet. I had a heavy pocketful of change since everything below a five-pound note is coinage. Thankfully one fit perfectly into the slot.

Chasing the Lost Dream

When my train arrived I boarded, found a seat, and waited the fifteen minutes before departure. The trip took about forty-five minutes, and I actually recognized that we were getting close when all I could see were rolling hills of green. Even though I was sure of the stop I left the train with a certain amount of trepidation that I couldn't explain. I walked out onto the sidewalk from the crowded parking lot.

I looked down the road towards the village of Otford. I could see nothing but picket fences, well-manicured lawns and the roofs of a few houses, most with chimneys. The bend in the road blocked any view of the town I remembered, a lifetime ago with Paul.

With adrenaline pumping through my system I trudged up the hill, my numb fingertips barely holding onto the luggage being dragged behind me. I turned right onto Coombe Road, the street my friends live on. For a split second I wished I had been born a mountain goat. I felt that it was the only way I could ascend that hill without a heart attack. I walked slowly but arrived huffing and puffing, barely able to speak a word by the time I knocked on their door.

Andrea greeted me at the side door with a hug and strong arms to keep me from falling over like I had just been sucker-punched. Before the door closed behind me two young hellions came running out from someplace beyond the kitchen to greet the visitor. Cameron was around five. He was tall and slender and since he had been in school for a couple of years, had the typical British accent, already sounding a little snooty. Graeme was younger and built solidly like a pint-sized truck driver with his pants at half-mast.

Cameron remembered me but was shy and answered my questions with either a yes or a no, never going into details. Graeme immediately wanted me to know his entire life history

Digging In

with whatever limited vocabulary he had. Fortunately it was a short history since he was only three.

I had no sooner sat down at the kitchen table than Andrea handed me a package from the Archaeological Society of Britain. Eager fingers pulled apart the plain brown paper wrapping. I spread all the pamphlets on the table and discovered that it was exactly the same packet that had arrived in Canada just before I left. It contained information on joining the society, along with an application, exactly what the society did, and where the donated money would be spent. What I had hoped for was an invitation to work at one of the digs. Not only was there no invitation, there wasn't even a list of where the digs were taking place. There was no information that would get me started or at least head me off in the right direction. Andrea could see by the look on my face that I was expecting more. She said nothing.

Before I could get too comfortable or allow jet lag to take hold and dump me onto the closest unoccupied couch, we loaded the kids into the car and went off to Tesco's, one of the larger grocery store chains in Sevenoaks, about thirty minutes away.

Everything in the thirteenth century town had stayed the same as I had remembered. It was all so familiar that I had to fight back the tears. The entire planet had remained the same. Only my world had been turned upside down. In that split second I wondered if I had done the right thing by coming back, and the instant the thought popped into my mind I pushed it out.

Andrea purchased some fruit and vegetables, a huge tub of vanilla ice cream, chocolate sauce, whipping cream, chopped walnuts and a large jar of red maraschino cherries. There were other things that went into the basket but nothing that sparked my imagination quite like the mountain of hot fudge ice cream sundae that I was planning for myself.

Chasing the Lost Dream

I picked up a bottle of red wine and laid it carefully in a corner of the basket. It was at that precise moment that Andrea told me that she wasn't drinking these days. She was three-months pregnant.

"Well, I'm not," I announced. "I'm sure Phil (her husband) isn't either. So you lose. We'll drink it ourselves," I said with a bit of a snicker.

We stopped at the fabric store to pick up some quilting pieces and several brightly colored felt squares. On the way home we stopped at the butcher shop in Otford to pick up lamb chops for dinner and ground beef to restock her freezer. By the time we arrived home, with her completed list of stops, we were exhausted; Andrea from her nonstop schedule, with two small boys and a household to run, her pregnancy and constant nausea and me from an overnight, constantly interrupted flight and almost no sleep. We busied ourselves the minute we walked through the door.

Andrea, the boys and myself ate dinner around six. Phil didn't come home from work until after eight. I kept him company while he ate. Andrea gave the boys their bath and by nine was ready for bed herself.

"Oh, by the way," she said, "I forgot to tell you. Get a good night's sleep. I signed you up for a dig starting tomorrow morning. If the boys don't wake you first I'll wake you at six."

I was stunned.....delighted.....but stunned!

Chapter 5

Day One of the Rest of my Life

Despite the excitement of an archaeological dream-come-true I slept like the dead through most of the night, but was awake long before Andrea came knocking on the door. I could hear the kids giggling in the television room, but my fear of having to listen to non-stop jabbering so early in the morning kept me confined to the only ground floor bedroom.

There was time for a quick cup of coffee with loads of milk to cool it down, and a couple of slices of buttered toast with peanut butter and jelly before I was out the door. Andrea handed me a brown paper sack; while making my way down the almost vertical driveway, I took a quick peek inside. She had fixed lunch for me.

I walked to the house two-doors to the right, a red-brick cottage covered in ivy, in the center of the cul-de-sac. Elizabeth Ward, an elegant-looking woman in her fifties, dressed casually in camel-colored slacks and a dark brown sweater, was standing in the doorway. She was anxious to be on her way and stood there, hat-in-hand, so to speak. There wasn't really time for pleasantries and I assumed we would get acquainted along the way. I was wrong. The dig was taking place within a couple of miles from their Coombe Road home and there was barely enough time to buckle myself in, check the landscape and the direction in which we were headed, before we were pulling into the Latimers' driveway. Without fanfare Elizabeth introduced me to my work mates.

The day started with a morning briefing that I discovered would be a ritual at every dig. Jill and Amanda and myself sat listening to the events of the previous few days, and I

Chasing the Lost Dream

learned how and why The Archaeological Society of Kent was called in.

"The Latimers had been digging up part of their garden to put in a walkway leading to what would be a tennis court when they discovered what they thought was an ancient Roman coin," Elizabeth explained. "They called us, as is required by law for any change in the land, and gave us one week to complete our investigation."

Elizabeth, feeling that she was leaving me in capable hands, told me that she would be back early in the afternoon. She thanked me and left. I was feeling only slightly abandoned.

Jill was in her mid-twenties. She was rather plain looking, even with round tortoise-shell glasses that should have added a bit of mystery to her looks but didn't. Her khaki shorts with lots of pockets and matching tee shirt did nothing to hide a stocky, physically fit body. Her hair had a tinge of auburn and was short and straight with bangs that covered her eyebrows, giving her that startled 'deer-in-the-headlights' look. Her skin, from hours in what little sun was available, had a slight tan to it.

Amanda was closer to my height, probably around five-six or seven. She was leaner, with not quite so evident muscles. She looked to be in her late thirties, with a few strands of gray mixed in with the long brown wavy hair that was pulled back in a low ponytail.

Both women were friendly, talkative and efficient as we dug a foot-wide trench around a twelve-foot square block of flat stones. Amanda cut sod while Jill and I carried and emptied buckets heavy with loose earth a close distance from where we were digging. With a long-handled broom and then a short, stubby whisk I swept the area clean of every bit of debris.

Jill and Amanda were kneeling for hours, their noses as close to the ground as is humanly possible without actually touching, checking for the subtle changes that they tried to point

Digging In

out to me but I couldn't see. We found shards of pottery, fired flint and metal pieces. There was nothing large enough to get me as excited as they were.

The work was backbreaking, knee-crushing, abs-crunching, and arm-lengthening as if being pulled out of their sockets. There was nothing pleasant about it but I was glad for the physical pain rather than the emotional pain that came with the first anniversary of the death of my husband on this day.

I was delighted when Elizabeth and her daughter Helen picked me up around one o'clock. "If tomorrow is the first day of the rest of my life," I said to anyone within earshot who would listen, "it's only fair that I start it off racked with physical pain."

"Well then," said Elizabeth showing no sympathy whatsoever, "it can only get better."

She dropped me off right at the bottom of the Webb's driveway. I looked up at the twenty-percent grade to the back door and wondered if I had the strength to make it. I waved at Elizabeth and Helen, sure that I heard my shoulder joint squeak like a rusty metal gate, and turned to the task at hand. I had to conquer my own personal Mount Everest, knowing full well that my arms and legs objected strenuously to what I had subjected them to most of the day. By the time my aching fingers gripped the door handle, and were too sore to turn the knob, I wanted to cry. I guess Andrea heard me fumbling with the doorknob and opened the door for me. I was so grateful even though she just stood there laughing, reminding me that this is what I wanted to do for the summer.

We talked about our day while she prepared dinner. In the sink I soaked my hands in warm, soapy water, massaging my fingers until moving them felt bearable. I was sure that I could now hold onto eating utensils.

Chasing the Lost Dream

I spent a quiet evening with Andrea who did some needlecraft work while we watched television. We talked a little about what I really wanted to do for the summer. The dig would be over within the week. I was less sure now than when I first arrived about what I wanted to do with the next several months, since every minor move produced a plethora of pain.

I took a long, hot bath and went to bed early thinking I would once again sleep like I had done the night before.

I was wrong!

Chapter 6

Ups and (Way) Downs

It was an endless night of tossing and turning.

My tall, broad-shouldered, blond (with a full-lip strawberry-red mustache that looked so perfect on his sweet face) husband just stood there on the beach looking out over the water, the tiny waves lapping at his bare feet, like I had seen so many times before. The events of our all-too-few years together played over and over like a phonograph needle stuck in a groove.

While I slept Paul came to life in my dream, and as long as he was there, all I could feel was the total contentment that came with being near him, looking at him, talking to him. We walked along the beach, our fingers intertwined and exploring. The warm sand was under our feet on one of our favorite beaches on the tropical island of Tobago. The granulated sand that I scooped up and let flow through my fingers brought his hands closer to catch the steady stream before it returned to the beach. The whisper of the swaying palm fronds made me feel that we were alone and could share our innermost thoughts and dreams. We couldn't see or hear the cars that whizzed by on the road just beyond the trees but I knew they were there.

Without knowing why, the dream suddenly changed. Paul and I were sitting at a picnic table in a little town in Vermont. We both looked up as the town clock struck three. We talked as we always did about little things and nothing at all. When I reached for his hand I was jolted awake.

I was alone in the dark, not knowing where I was and not caring. I wanted desperately to get back to sleep. I wanted

Chasing the Lost Dream

to see him again.....to touch him. My body was aching to wrap around him.

I was suddenly wide-awake. Every bone, every joint, every muscle screamed in pain. I lay back on my pillow and cried until I fell asleep and the dreams started all over again.

*   *   *   *

Andrea smiled at me over her coffee cup. She knew by my eyes that I hadn't slept well but made no comment.

"If you can," she said quietly, "why don't you try to take a nap this morning while I take the boys shopping. We're going to a party this afternoon and I need a few munchies." They left right after breakfast.

I was grateful for the time alone and stretched out on the couch with the television set all to myself, droning softly in the background. I fell asleep almost immediately and slept dreamlessly until I heard the back door open. The boys came charging into the room, each wanting to show me the toy that mummy had bought for them because they had been good. They had been gone for a couple of hours, and my undisturbed nap took the edge off the depression that had threatened to overwhelm me.

Phil fixed a hamburger and hot dog barbecue lunch that we ate on paper plates in the back yard. Even the boys were quiet while they ate and I don't think anyone realized how much I appreciated it. When the spoils from lunch were bunched up and thrown into a big, black garbage bag we were ready to head out to the party at the Todman's, just a couple of miles away. I was certainly ready for some fun. The ride was short but the boys were rambunctious and loud so I was glad when we arrived, my sanity intact.

Digging In

I was introduced to about nine or ten people, and despite the fact that Paul and I had met many of the Webbs' friends and acquaintances over our years of visiting, none of these people looked even slightly familiar. I knew that everyone in the group was married to another member in the group but I couldn't figure out who was with whom.

There were bunches of kids of various ages, shapes and sizes, but since the backyard was large and fully enclosed no one seemed to worry about them. Within minutes all the kids were deeply engrossed in playing some sort of soccer that they referred to as 'footie-ball.'

I helped Andrea unpack her picnic hamper, and couldn't believe that my quiet, sensitive, elegant friend had packed two spray cans of rancid whipped cream just in case the party got dull.

"Andrea," I said, "I can understand one can going bad. Where did you get two cans of rancid whipped cream?"

"Well," she replied "I like buying in bulk and occasionally things just end up lost at the back of a cupboard or the refrigerator. Besides, you never know when you're going to be called upon to liven things up."

Andrea didn't wait for things to get dull. It was late afternoon. We had nibbled to our hearts' content from platters of canapés and sandwich quarters, bowls of nuts and pretzels and bags of crisps. The party was very much in full swing when Andrea, a glint in her eye that meant trouble was coming, called me into the kitchen. We armed ourselves: we took the safety valve off both cans, tested them in the kitchen sink, and came out spraying. We headed straight for the kids. Seeing the foamy spray coming at them from familiar-looking cans stopped them dead in their tracks. They tried to catch the whipped cream with their hands and mouth until they realized how gross it tasted. Shrieking with laughter, they ran helter-

Chasing the Lost Dream

skelter through the yard. We gave chase. By the time we were out of whipped cream we were out of breath from laughing and running. The kids continued to run wild in the yard so we left them.

Andrea and I and a couple of the other women retreated to the kitchen to help with the clean up. The men picked up all the bits and pieces that had been scattered from one end of the yard to the other and packed them, making sure their kids had all their clothes, toys and other paraphernalia that they had come with.

Phil packed the trunk with the kids' stuff, and the instant Cameron and Graeme calmed down ever so slightly, they were whisked into the car and buckled into their car seats. Within minutes we were headed for home and arrived around seven. While Andrea flipped on the television and put her aching, swollen feet up on a hassock, Phil stripped the boys, dumped them both into the tub and gave them a bath.

I excused myself and went to the Wards' house to find out about the dig. There was no time to relax. I was handed a bunch of old toothbrushes and a pail of ice-cold water, and was instantly roped into helping them clean and wash the finds from the day at the dig.

By the time I got back to the Webbs' house the boys and Andrea were fast asleep and Phil was watching television.

I thanked him for the terrific day!

Chapter 7

Time to Move On.....

Elizabeth rousted me up and out of the house the next morning by tooting the horn from the bottom of the driveway. I was grateful that most of my aches and pains were under control, thanks to some over-the-counter painkillers that I had tucked away in my luggage. I sidestepped down to her car with relative ease.

I worked that day with Elizabeth and Ben, Amanda's sixteen-year-old son. Ben was tall and slender with coloring similar to his mother and definitely on his way to being an archaeologist. He was a very serious young man who didn't talk unless he was spoken to, and even then it was only about the findings at the dig.

After a quick introduction there was no time for chitchat. Ben and I leveled the one-foot deep moat that surrounded the 'floor' of the dig with small shovels and short-handled brooms. We swept away bits of debris that had accumulated on the stones. Since we had done that before I correctly assumed that the site was swept every workday. Within minutes Elizabeth measured the outer perimeter of the work area. Before I left the dig site was covered with a large blue tarp. Nothing more would be done that day.

We were home by noon. I was glad that there wasn't much in the way of heavy-duty manual labor because my still tender body would have screamed obscenities at me and probably shut down in protest. As it was, my body whispered softly that it was ready for a major career change.

Chasing the Lost Dream

I spent the rest of the afternoon helping Andrea with cleaning and laundry, and since twice the help made for half the work we finished in record time. We both relaxed before dinner and took a short nap in front of the television set, she in her favorite lounge chair with her feet up on a matching ottoman, and I sprawled out on the couch with a pillow from my bed supporting my head.

The last day at the dig was Tuesday the twenty-ninth of June. I, the sole remaining crew member, swept away the debris for the last time. It was now time for Elizabeth to complete the work. Each stone was measured and mapped out on graph paper. The site was then photographed from every angle. When the measuring was finished each stone was lifted to check underneath. Nothing of significance was found.

Since it was almost noon the four of us (Elizabeth and myself, joined by her daughter Helen and her husband Cliff) walked up the main street of Otford to the Red Lion pub for a fish and chip celebration lunch. We returned to the site early afternoon to finish the inspection, and for Elizabeth to write up her notes for the Archaeological Society of Kent, and a 'thank you' card to the Latimers.

Cliff drove us back to their home where I spent an hour with them having tea and biscuits and thanking them for the unique 'dig' experience. I then enjoyed a quiet evening with Phil and Andrea.

*   *   *   *

I awoke filled with dread. I was leaving the cocoon that my friends had provided so graciously. It was a travel day that I was not looking forward to, and no amount of chitchat over coffee and toast would calm my jittery nerves.

26

Digging In

Along with my luggage and a brown-bag lunch that Andrea prepared and packed for me, we drove to the train station in time to get the first train of the day going to Cardiff, Wales. I purchased a one-way ticket from the stationmaster. We said our good-byes and she gave me a hug for luck. She knew just by looking at me that I was terrified, and I hoped that she couldn't feel me shaking. Within minutes of our hug I boarded the train which left almost immediately. When I looked back at the platform from my window seat Andrea was gone and I felt a momentary jolt in the pit of my stomach.

The trip was pleasant and the weather warm and sunny, which should have lifted my spirits. I tried to read but couldn't concentrate, and there was no one to talk to. Just before the arrival in Cardiff I ate the ham and cheese sandwich that somehow had been squashed in transit. The apple was intact and despite the fact that I couldn't taste much, it added a little saliva to my dry mouth.

I arrived late morning and made my way over to the Tourist Information Center located just down the way from the train station. With the help of the woman behind the desk and a rather crude map that she gave me I found my way to GRE Insurance office on the main street. It was the company that had originally insured the van for my husband.

They went over the paperwork. They would insure my van for the sum of three hundred and twelve pounds (approximately six hundred and twenty-five Canadian dollars). I breathed a sigh of relief that they would insure me but gasped at the cost.

The bank was closed for the day.....I wasn't sure why. I told the agent at the insurance company that I would return the next day with cash, but that I needed the coverage today so I could get my van out of storage. The amount I would be paying for insurance did not cover my van if an accident was my fault.

Chasing the Lost Dream

That coverage would have brought the total up to over a thousand Canadian dollars and I didn't feel that it was worth it.

From Cardiff I took the train for the short hop to the Barry Docks. I arrived in early afternoon, and strolled the short distance from the train station to where my van had been parked for the past year. I walked into the old and rather shabby-looking storage rental office and was greeted by an office assistant sitting behind stacks of paperwork.

The manager, Roger Bennett, was called over the intercom. He came out to the lobby, greeting me with a warm two-handed handshake. I had written to him about Paul's death and asked if he wouldn't mind looking after the van until I could get back. He had replied with a letter of condolence and a promise to do whatever he could to help. We talked briefly in his office, but I was anxious to see the van and he knew it.

While I fidgeted he called a local garage where I could get the van serviced, the oil changed and a MOT sticker applied to the front window, which would guarantee that the vehicle was road-worthy. I know that when I was out of the office for a few minutes Roger had explained the situation to the garage manager.

I went out to start the van that I had only driven once or twice before, but never comfortably. I could feel my insides shaking like I had spent the entire morning downing a gallon of strong coffee. After a year of sitting dormant even the doors of the van objected to my intrusion.

I sat for a moment not moving, not even breathing. Finally I stuck the key in place and turned. The battery let out a low, barely audible growl. I tried again, listening to the same noise, and then again. With each turn of the key it sounded stronger and louder but it needed that spark. Just about the time the tears were ready to flow and a scream threatened to escape

Digging In

through my gritted teeth and clenched jaw there was an 'almost caught' sound. One last try and it roared to life!

I took a deep, somewhat satisfying, breath for the first time since getting behind the wheel. I gave the van some gas and let it idle. A minute or two later, when I put it in first gear and tried to move, it died. It re-started immediately and I kept it running with my foot trembling on the gas pedal.

I hoped I had enough gas to make it to the service station!

Chapter 8

Panic

While the van was gasping and sputtering and trying to wake up from its year-long coma Roger came out to see how I was doing. "If they can't finish the servicing today," he said, "you can bring the van back here and stay in it overnight. We'll lock you in the enclosed yard so you'll feel safe."

I smiled meekly, thanked him then drove the van through the gate and out onto the streets of Barry, a community long past its prime and made all the more sinister due to its proximity to the docks. I could feel my leg trembling on the gas pedal. The thought of camping all alone in a locked compound with no one close enough to hear me if I yelled for help did nothing to ease my tension. I prayed every inch of the way that it wouldn't die or run out of gas or make some ungodly sound that I wouldn't recognize before I got to the service station even though the service station was actually spitting distance. I knew that in a matter of minutes I could have walked all the way to the garage and gotten help if I needed it. I breathed a sigh of relief when I pulled right in front of the bay door and turned off the ignition.

I introduced myself to the garage manager and handed him the keys. He drove the van inside where the mechanics went to work on it immediately. The oil and filter were changed and whatever was supposed to be lubed I assumed was lubed. The inspection was finished in record time. I don't think they inspected it too closely.

In a way I was grateful for the speed with which the job was done; and yet a tiny part of my brain went into overdrive

Digging In

wondering what they had missed and how secure I should feel driving.

The manager insisted upon having the van washed. The outside of the van was a mess with the chocolate brown-on-beige coloring looking more like a dappled, smudged, and all-around sooty gray. The windows were coated in a sticky film that water and the wipers did nothing to clear away. The offer was very kind, and I knew it, but I was edgy and more than a little nauseous from anxiety and fatigue. The manager kept talking non-stop and I had trouble understanding his accent, so I just kept nodding and smiling and gritting my teeth to the point that my jaw ached.

It was late afternoon and I could see the sun was just starting to go down. The thought of driving and trying to find the campground in the dark in a city the size of Cardiff terrified me but I couldn't refuse his offer. I had no way of cleaning the outside of the van myself, and trying to see through the dingy windshield would have been impossible when the sun went down.

Although the camper had been out in the open, without a tree in sight, it was covered from front to back bumper with some kind of sticky sap. On my own, and without benefit of a compartment full of cleaning products and buckets of hot water, I would have found impossible to remove. It was harder still, and far more imperative, to get whatever the substance was off the windshield.

They used a high-powered hose, liquid detergent and long-handled scrubbing brushes. The manager, while directing the work, kept talking and talking and talking like an out-of-control robot until I wanted to cover my ears with the palms of my hands. I just wanted to get out of there and the longer he talked the less I listened. The more anxious I became the less I understood his incessant chatter. The minute they turned off the

Chasing the Lost Dream

hose I excused myself and went to dry off the windows with a large towel I found in one of the cupboards in the van.

I thanked him profusely, paid the bill which was a lot less than I would have paid had Roger not called, and jumped into the van after being given directions to town. All three assured me that the road was well marked. The camper roared to life like it was ready for the next adventurous chapter in its life. I drove it out onto the main street.

The drive was hellishly slow. There were stop signs at every corner on the eight-mile drive and I could feel the beginning of panic, as the sun set lower in the sky. My mouth tasted sour. My hands were clutching the steering wheel so tightly my fingers cramped, and the gas pedal quivered under my shaking foot. My left arm and shoulder ached from having to shift gears continually and with the wrong hand. I forced myself to breathe slowly and evenly. I tried desperately to calm down but I was losing the battle.

I cursed Paul for leaving me.....for making me fend for myself when I didn't want to. Where was he when I needed him.....and I needed him all the time!

I was sure that once I saw Cardiff Castle, that loomed over the center of the city, I would know where to go. Paul and I had camped there on more than one occasion. I just needed to get there.

Each mile seemed to be a torturous eternity. I had to just keep driving, slow and steady. I concentrated on the road but nothing looked even vaguely familiar. It was all so confusing and my mind was in such turmoil. The signs said straight ahead to Cardiff – 'seven miles,' then 'six miles.' "Oh my God," a voice screamed inside my head, "what happens if I get lost in Cardiff?" Please let me just get there – 'four miles.' Please let me get there and I'll be okay – 'two miles.' "Please

Digging In

don't let me get lost," I prayed over and over and over, tears that I wouldn't let fall stinging my eyes.

I rounded one of the street corners and there it was – Cardiff Castle. It towered like a giant over the entire city. It was visible from every downtown street and I was so grateful. I could suddenly hear myself gasping for breath, and then slowly.....very slowly.....for the first time.....I closed my mouth and breathed deeply through my nose.

I drove directly towards the Castle, and smiled meekly when I saw all the stone animals crouching on the wall ready to pounce. I drove around to the back and took one of the side streets into the campground.

The office was closed but I didn't care!

Chapter 9

My Port in the Storm

I let my eyes, stinging with tears and fatigue and fear, scrutinize the campground. I could see a mishmash of mini-motorhomes and trailers and tents scattered about the place but thankfully there were still many vacant camping spots. I pulled into a fairly level one close to the bathhouse. I turned the key to off and before I could stop myself my shoulders hunched, and my head, too filled with pain to keep up a second longer, dropped to the steering wheel. Clutching the only source of strength I could hold onto I broke down, my fingers gripping the wheel for dear life.

Relief at finding a place to camp, anger at being stupid enough to be in a foreign country alone, sick at heart over the death of my beautiful, young husband, and total exhaustion from not sleeping and still sore from the dig or perhaps everything rolled into one, the roller coaster of emotions swallowed me.

"Oh my God, how am I going to manage this all by myself!" the thought whispered in my head and escaped with my breath in unintelligible mumbles. I had a three-month, non-refundable airline ticket that I had forced onto myself so I wouldn't change my mind.

I don't know how long I cried. I just cried until I was empty. When I was finally exhausted and tired of feeling sorry for myself and had taken a few deep, calming breathes, I dried my face as best I could. I used the same towel to wipe my face that I had used to wipe the windows, and I felt better because it was still moist and cool and only slightly smelly.

Digging In

I plugged in the van and turned the refrigerator on, hoping it still worked. I went into the washroom to clean up a little. I blew my nose, washed my face and hands with warm, soapy water and dried myself with Paul's favorite orange bath towel that I found in one of the under-the-seat compartments. When I felt I could pass inspection I walked back towards my van, stopping to talk with a couple who were sitting outside their trailer. After a few pleasantries I asked if they knew where I could find a grocery store that might still be open.

It was almost six o'clock, the refrigerator was empty, and I needed to keep busy. I also needed some little thing to eat and some coffee for the morning. The couple directed me to a small, local grocery store, within walking distance. I thanked them and left.

I had to eat something even though my stomach was still in a knot and my head was pounding. I found the shop at the end of the second block. I bought a couple of buns, a tomato, a block of white cheese, a slab of butter, instant coffee, a small box of sugar cubes, and a container of milk. I walked back to the van in the rapidly fading light.

Once the sandwich was made and I took my first bite, the tears returned. I could force myself to swallow only a few mouthfuls.

I wrapped up the sandwich in some waxed paper and put it in the refrigerator that was just starting to chill. I dragged the moist towel across my face again, paying extra attention to my red-rimmed eyes, then grabbed a bottle of wine that I had found in one of the cupboards and went out the back door.

I knocked on the trailer door of the couple who had given me directions to the grocery store. The lady of the house opened the door and promptly invited me in. As I passed her she peeked out and around the door saying "Oh, are you alone?"

Chasing the Lost Dream

With that innocent remark the floodgates opened again. Instinctively her arm went around my shoulder protectively. She motioned to her husband to get me a brandy. "There! There!" she said, "you're all right now. You're with friends." When I sat down at the table he handed me a drink and it seemed an eternity before I could get myself under control enough to tell my hosts my problem.

They introduced themselves as June and Gil and said they were waiting for a friend living in the neighborhood to come by for a drink. When I tried to excuse myself so I wouldn't intrude they wouldn't hear of it.

"Not to fear," June announced, "there's lots of brandy to go around and if we run out we'll open bottles of wine. You'll enjoy Nia. She's wonderfully amusing."

By the time Nia arrived, smartly dressed in navy blue business clothes, my weeps were over. Over a sweet dessert she told us about the people at her government job. By the time we finished a couple of bottles of wine the hilarious stories, theirs and a few of mine, had put us all in a much more relaxed mood. Over peanuts, pretzels and crisps we talked and laughed late into the night. The evening ended with one last brandy that finished the bottle and an invitation from Nia. Breakfast would be served at her flat early the next morning.

Nia and I left together. I thanked and hugged my hosts for the wonderful evening. I retrieved my bath towel and a bar of soap from the van and hurried to the empty bathhouse. I smiled as I relived some of the wild stories I had just heard. My shower lasted much longer than I anticipated as I drained the hot water tank, letting the running water wash all the tension away. By the end of it I was feeling somewhat sober, much cleaner and more relaxed than I had at any time during the entire day, possibly the entire week.

Digging In

With all the wine and brandy in my system I knew I would sleep well!

Chapter 10

A Day With Promise

Thanks to the help of my new-found friends, more brandy than I had consumed in my lifetime, interesting lighthearted conversation along with knowing that I had something to do in the morning, and a couple of pain pills to relieve the potential hangover, I managed to sleep through most of the night without too much tossing and turning. I could not have tossed and turned even if I wanted to since I had not put all the cushions together to make a double bed; I had slept on the seats on one side of the camper with my back up against the wall. I felt okay when I got out of bed around the time that the sun was coming up.

I dressed in my black track pants and a long sleeved light blue turtleneck sweater because of the dampness. I folded up my bedding slowly since it still wasn't fully light and I needed to kill all the time I could. I boiled the water for some instant coffee and put my feet up on the second bed while I drank it, trying to act casual even though I didn't feel that way. When I was through fussing, I went out to pay for a couple of nights of camping, since I saw that the office lights had come on while I was having my coffee. They were ready for business and welcomed me warmly.

I stopped by Gil and June's camper and they were ready to head out the door. I thanked them again for helping me through the evening before. We walked the few blocks to Nia's cottage without much talking.

After a relaxing brunch with sliced meats, a variety of cheeses, a fresh fruit cup and strong, freshly brewed coffee, followed by a stroll through Nia's small English garden we all

Digging In

said goodbye. It was mid-morning; Nia left for work and June and Gil went back to the campground. I walked to downtown Cardiff and spent the rest of the morning walking around the city taking care of many necessary items of personal business.

I got the van 'road taxed' (licensed). I closed my account at Barclay's Bank and removed the last of my British Sterling that had remained from the previous year. I went back to the GRE Insurance Company and paid cash for my vehicle insurance. Paying that bill took care of most of the money that had been left in the account. The fact that I was a foreigner and a woman made highway robbery legal where insurance was concerned. I resented it right down to my bone marrow. Since I didn't take out liability insurance, I hoped that any accident I was involved in wouldn't be my fault. I hoped that I wouldn't have an accident.....period!

Much of the afternoon was spent at the Archaeological Society of Cardiff. The Archaeological Society had its office in the museum. While I waited to see someone in charge I wandered up one side of the enormous room and down the other side. The walls on both sides were lined with paintings by the masters, and large, marble statues covered much of the floor space. I stopped to study each and every one without really concentrating on any of them. At every stop I prayed silently that there would be a dig going on close to Cardiff where I could volunteer my services. I did not want to drive anywhere.

After trudging from office to office, filling out a couple of application forms and wandering the museum for hours, I learned that they did not need any more volunteers at any of the dig sites but they would keep my application on file if something became available. There was no phone number or address that I could give them. I had hoped for the impossible.....an immediate acceptance.

Chasing the Lost Dream

I was disappointed but refused to allow myself to sink any deeper into depression. I hoped that the tears that stung my eyes didn't dribble down my cheek and betray me. I really didn't know what I would do next because I had counted on something coming through from the museum.

"I am a survivor," I said over and over under my breath. "I'll get through this," I whimpered. I bit my lower lip so I wouldn't cry. I left the building and walked slowly down the main street hoping something would come to me.

It was late afternoon when I wandered back to the campground. June and Gil had left along with several other campers and no one was sitting outside any of the parked camping vehicles. I flung open the side door of my camper. I took the now stale sandwich, complete with bite marks on part of the bun, out of the refrigerator. While it warmed to room temperature I made myself another cup of coffee and sat at the table and ate. When I couldn't bite off a hunk of sandwich because it was as hard as a rock I dunked it into the hot coffee. It became soggy but palatable.

It was close to dark when I found a pay phone and called my friends in Temple Cloud, twelve miles south of Bristol. Barb Webb, the distaff side of the couple that shared the house with my friends, answered the phone. Although Bill and Jean Higgs were not at home Barb sounded like she knew all about me and was expecting my call.

Barb, or her husband Glynn, would welcome me if the Higgs were not home when I arrived.

I was relieved to hear and talk to a friendly voice but I would now have to drive the van more than seventy-five miles to see them. I had driven it less than ten miles so far and was not the least bit comfortable behind the wheel.

Before I was even off the phone I started to panic. My mind exploded into a hundred different directions like a movie

Digging In

being fast-forwarded. I had no idea where the highways were or even how to get out of Cardiff. I would have to read a map while driving and find my way through the heart of Bristol, a major sized city. I would be driving on the wrong side of the road, sitting on the wrong side of the van and shifting with the wrong hand. Within seconds of putting the telephone receiver back in its cradle I was terrified. I was depressed. There was no one to turn to for help.

For the hundredth time I chided myself over the stupidity of this undertaking. It was total lunacy and it had hardly begun. I could suddenly hear my heart pounding as it threatened to jump out of my chest. I was taking short gasping breaths. Hyperventilating had not been unusual for me in the past year. My shoulders slumped as I carried the weight of the world back to my camper in the dark.

Without friends to talk to and wine or brandy to dull the pain I did not sleep well. I awoke with each toss and turn. Sometime in the middle of the night two chairs and a table came crashing down from an overhead rack narrowly missing my head.

"I'll have to start selling things off," I told myself in the wee hours of the morning. "The round, plastic table that we bought in Spain for Paul's birthday, a couple of canvas folding chairs that we purchased at a market in France, the bicycle rack that we had brought with us from Canada, the radio we had purchased in Gibraltar, and Paul's golf clubs and bag will all have to go," I said to myself. "When the camper van is 'mine' rather than 'ours' it'll have to be sold also." I wanted the van to be used, not stored for months at a time, sitting idle and rusting away.

It was much too early to think about but I knew in my heart that I would not be happy traveling alone, and I didn't want anyone else with me in the van that I had shared with the

41

man I loved. I tried pushing all these thoughts that had plagued me during this first year of widowhood to the back of my mind. "I'm between a rock and a hard place" and "this is a catch-22 situation," were just a few of my favorite expressions that kept popping into my mind.

I had never been a crier and I hated the way I felt. I tried desperately to hold back the tears, but every new situation opened the floodgates to anger and frustration and unbearable sadness.

I was relieved when the sun finally started to come up and I didn't have to lay there in the dark with my mind creating problems for me that weren't there yet. After coffee and the second hard-as-a-rock bun with butter I wandered around the campground until I found someone who could give me directions to get out of Cardiff. A rather pleasant-looking, gray-haired woman on her way back from the washroom was happy to oblige. I followed her back to her trailer, and after a brief explanation, her husband wrote the directions out for me. They seemed easy enough, without too many turns.

I cleaned up the camper, putting everything back in its proper place, hoping things would stay put during the drive. I made sure all the cupboards were closed securely and checked all the drawers because I remembered that they would frequently pop open when Paul hit a bump in the road.

I screwed up my courage, got behind the wheel of the van and left the campground around mid-morning, hoping that I had missed the early rush-hour traffic jams. With every mile of driving I gained a little more confidence. The city roads were clearly marked with directions for getting to the highway. I was grateful for the written directions but I hadn't really needed them.

I actually relaxed a bit driving the motorway and released the death grip I had on the steering wheel. By early

Digging In

afternoon I had arrived in Bristol. There was little traffic on the road. Slowly and carefully I made my way through the city and found the A37 heading south. I did not have to look for highway signs since the large, white route numbers were painted on the road in two of the lanes, and I had highlighted the map in brilliant, canary yellow so there was no way I could miss them.

This was almost too easy and I was so grateful!

Chapter 11

Reminiscing

My telephone call was transferred to Jean and Bill. They were stunned when I announced that I was calling from a variety shop at the north end of Temple Cloud, a town consisting of one main street with a store or two sitting on either side of the post office. There were also a few side streets with homes on them, and lots of gently rolling open pasture surrounding the hamlet of Temple Cloud. Jean knew exactly where I was and couldn't believe that I had made it that far without numerous panicky telephone calls. She and Bill had been willing to come get me and lead me to their home from as far away as Bristol, should it have been necessary.

Over a static-filled connection they directed me to East Court Road, and cautioned me to drive very slowly because as I headed south on the main street it was an almost invisible entrance with no street name or markings that made any sense.

I spotted the dirt road turnoff with overhanging tree limbs (and no other markings) just as I was about to drive past. I turned left onto the exaggerated cow path and then left again almost immediately onto East Court Road. Unfortunately, I had forgotten to ask and Jean had forgotten to mentioned, how far along East Court Road I was to drive. I drove slowly looking on both sides for the two-storey brick building covered with ivy.

I should have trusted my friends!

I could see from a distance that there was a crowd standing in the middle of the one-and-a-half lane roadway. Jean and Bill, and Barb and her daughter Abby were all standing there waving and cheering. I could not have been more proud of myself if I had skyrocketed to the moon.

Digging In

As I approached I could see Bill making hand and arm gestures as if directing the landing of a 747, as he pointed the way towards their driveway. I parked my van beside his motorhome at the bottom of the hill and quickly ran back up for a hug from my friends and an introduction to Barb.

I soon discovered that although Barb had greeted me like a long-lost friend the evening before she had had no idea who I was, where I had come from and how I had met the Higgs. She simply confused everyone by greeting them that way.

Over tea and biscuits I told the story. "Paul and I met Bill and Jean while camping at a boat club on the beach in Menton, France three years ago," I explained to Barb. "We became friends for the few days that we camped together and had exchanged addresses." That was really all the explanation she needed or cared about. Fortunately there was more to the story and whether she wanted to hear it or not I was prepared and eager to tell it.

I had seen Jean in Canada a couple of weeks before I left for this trip. She had been visiting relatives in Bath, Ontario and had called me. Sandra, my sister-in-law, had taken a message from Jean or Jane Higgs or Higgins, she couldn't remember which, and I called the number thinking that Sandra must have made a mistake and that I was calling a wrong number. I recognized Jean's accent the instant she spoke her first word, and I told her, rather excitedly, that I would be coming to England within a couple of weeks. She had no idea that Paul had died the year before and was stunned by the information relayed to her by Sandra.

The next day Jean took the train from Kingston (the closest major city to Bath) to downtown Toronto, then the bus heading north on Yonge Street and waited on the corner of Yonge and Bathurst. Within minutes of her arrival I picked her

Chasing the Lost Dream

up in my little red, two-seater Mazda truck. We spent the day together and had a great time traipsing around the Beaches area of downtown Toronto. "Now I'm here on your doorstep," I said. "Fair trade, I think."

While I told my story Jean, Barb and I finished our tea and cookies and, since it was well into the afternoon, did short work on a large bottle of wine. Although I had gone through various comfort levels, it was the first time I felt truly at ease since arriving in Britain.

I was welcome to stay as long as I wanted. Everyone in both families told me to stay. I was comfortable for the few days that I did stay. Once relaxed however it wasn't long before I slipped over the edge and became anxious.

I needed to spread my wings....or at least to flex them!

Chapter 12

The Visit

For the week that I spent with my friends in Temple Cloud I was wined and dined, entertained and encouraged. I could not have felt more love and devotion had I been royalty. I had my own bedroom on the third floor and could retire to my room whenever I felt like it. I never felt like being alone.

When I was exhausted from lack of sleep or just plain running around we turned on a movie or the television set and I promptly fell asleep stretched out on the couch exactly like I did at home. While I slept Jean dozed in her lounge chair, her knitting in a heap on her lap, her fingers still clutching the knitting needles.

Bill and Jean were both in their sixties. They were retired and loved having company. One of their favorite pastimes was getting into their motorhome with visiting friends and touring close to home. They lived in a beautiful area with lots of history, archaeological finds, quaint little villages, and pubs on every corner. Guests gave them a chance to see familiar sights through the eyes of a tourist.

On one of our day trips we drove out to Cheddar Gorge. The walls of the museum there were plastered with pictures of the nine-thousand-year-old skeleton dubbed "The Cheddar Man" that had been discovered in a cave in the year nineteen hundred and three. DNA tests had determined that a forty-two year-old history teacher, Adrian Taggett, living one kilometer from the cave was a direct descendant of The Cheddar Man. Further tests showed that The Cheddar Man suffered a violent death at the approximate age of twenty-three in the year seven thousand one hundred fifty B.C.

Chasing the Lost Dream

We all laughed when I commented that I couldn't see myself sitting still for nine days let alone nine thousand years like the one remaining living ancestor of The Cheddar Man, Adrian Taggett. "Perhaps he should have been born a tree," I said.

On another day we toured Wokey Hole, famous for the caverns. Unfortunately some local folks had fertilized the land with pig manure that weekend and we all gagged as we drove quickly through the countryside, never really enjoying our reason for being there.

After an hour or more of touring Wells Cathedral, where I purchased pencil sketches (reproductions, of course) of the exterior and the staircase inside the cathedral, we had lunch in the tearoom on the grounds before going outside into the garden that was in full bloom.

We spent part of the day walking around the ancient city of Bath. In the downtown area, where most of the tourists congregated, baskets of pink, red or white flowers hung from every lamppost and dripped water from the recent rain burst. After walking up and down many of the side streets we wandered into the museum. We went through the baths, not yet officially opened to the public due to the recent construction and sipped at the water from underground springs.

We browsed the gift shops but didn't stay long. We watched mimes, painted gold from head to toe and wearing white and gold long, flowing robes, guarding the front doors to the church.

On another day trip we stopped in Cornwall for an original Cornish pasty lunch and a cup of tea. I had already given them my opinion of a Cornish pasty but was assured that a Cornish pasty in Cornwall was totally different from Cornish pasties in other parts of England or the world. They were different.....but definitely not different enough or tasty enough

Digging In

to make me want to eat more than one.....even if I was starving to death.

We stopped at flea markets, street sales and antique shops just to see what they had available. My friends filled my every restless moment with interesting neighbors, friends and relatives, fascinating places.....and love.

I hadn't been there long enough to really get the accents down pat so when a friend of Glynn and Barb's showed up for an evening of pleasantries I sat and listened. I listened.....and listened.....and listened.....and not two words together did I understand. Just about the time I understood a couple of things he would be off on some tangent and I'd be lost again. I spent most of the evening lost. When he left and the conversation included only the people in the house I jokingly told Jean, "When I understand that guy it'll be time to go home."

Bill took one afternoon to check the oil in my van even though it had been changed when I had picked it up. He checked the water in the radiator, crawled under the van and inspected all the belts and hoses. We took it out for a ride to make sure it was running properly to Bill's well-tuned ear. Bill did the driving and assured me that it was in tiptop form.

*   *   *   *

Bill and Jean, Barb and Glynn could not have done more. They did everything to assure me that one day soon my life would be back to something close to normal and tolerable and even without a husband we would always be friends.

In quiet moments Jean listened to my innermost fears and thoughts and hopes and dreams. Almost every conversation ended in tears. She cried with me.

Something happens to people 'on a mission,' I thought. I had no idea what I was looking for. I certainly had no idea

Chasing the Lost Dream

what I would find. I just had to fill a tiny portion of the tremendous emptiness that had been left in my life. Paul's death had left an insatiable hunger that some unknown passion had to fill.

It was time to move on and look for it!

Chapter 13

My Home Away from Home

With so many friends and acquaintances in England I had put much thought and effort into 'guaranteeing' a relatively smooth transition into a solo life. I hoped that I wouldn't get too lonely there or spend too much time alone. In view of that, several weeks before leaving Canada I had written to friends Chris and Heidi Stevsen who owned a nursery specializing in rare and exotic plants near Colchester.

I called Heidi while I was with the Higgs and told her of my plans to head her way and "can you put me to work for a while?" I asked, mentally praying that she would say yes.

"There's always lots and lots of work to do so come along when you can," she said very enthusiastically. It never occurred to me that she was the spider luring the poor unsuspecting fly into her sticky maze of a web.

I left Jean and Bill's place knowing that I could return at anytime. It was an exhilarating feeling knowing that I could try it on my own, and if I just couldn't hack it a safety net would be there to catch me before I crash-landed. There wasn't one minute during the lunacy of those early months that I didn't feel grateful to these friends who swathed me in a protective cocoon.

One morning, feeling a little braver than usual, I got behind the wheel of my van with a heavily highlighted (in glowing canary-yellow) map on the seat beside me. My hands were firmly on the steering wheel. I started the van with a certain air of confidence that I reserved only for show. I drove up the driveway and out onto the road without even glancing back to see if anyone was watching. I waved a goodbye, knowing I was leaving the old 'me' behind.

Chasing the Lost Dream

In between Bristol and Colchester is Otford. I stopped for a day or two to visit my Canadian friends, Phil and Andrea Webb, who had arranged my first archaeological dig. Andrea did not seem to mind my popping in and out of her life like an out of control jack-in-the-box, and being totally outspoken I know that she would have said something if she did mind. With Phil working so many hours and commuting to and from downtown London I didn't see him much.

Andrea seemed thrilled with the fact that I would do all the cooking. Since her refrigerator was packed to overflowing I found myself inventing all kinds of things in the kitchen and, of course, I always made sure to use the whip cream on blueberries or strawberries, ice cream or just plain graham crackers before it went rancid.

I made little pizzas on crumpets with tomato sauce, shredded cheese and whatever vegetables she had 'fermenting' in the crisper. I baked muffins from boxes and boxes and boxes of mixes that she had on hand in case a marauding army stopped by needing sustenance. I put ingredients in salads, like chopped green olives, broccoli and cauliflower flowerets and sliced the stems into slivers before adding them. I shredded cheddar cheese to sprinkle on top, something Andrea wouldn't dream of using. I made vegetable spaghetti sauce from everything she had left on the bottom shelf of the refrigerator. I made homemade soup with a myriad of different shapes of noodles that were left in the bottom of countless bags and boxes that I found tucked away in the black corners of every shelf in the pantry. She would ask at every meal where I had found such-and-such and couldn't believe that they were in her cupboards.

Whatever I chose to do with my time and energy gave Andrea a little break from her routine and made me feel useful. I loved it. Andrea loved it. The kids, Cameron and Graeme,

Digging In

growing taller practically before my eyes, thought I was weird and took every opportunity to tell me so. They thought it strange that I arrived at odd times, moved in to the back bedroom for short periods of time, and then left. Sometimes I would leave before they awoke in the morning and when I showed up again they wanted to know where I had been and how long I would be staying this time. I didn't know how to answer them but they really weren't interested in the answer, I discovered, just in asking the question.

To add to my strangeness was the fact that I had the same funny accent as their mummy and daddy and that seemed to arouse their curiosity.

This time I stayed with my friends for three days. When the refrigerator needed restocking, the freezer packed with my cooked meals, and all the laundry had been washed, dried, folded and put away, I was eager to hit the road.

What surprised and delighted me most was the way I made my way around England. The route numbers were very clearly marked, even on the small, country roads. I had no trouble maneuvering through the narrow streets although I did drive very slowly much to the annoyance of the people following behind. At times the mirrors on the van touched bushes on both sides of the street. Somehow I always made it through without a scratch.

I repeated to myself more often than I cared to admit: "I am a survivor!"

Chapter 14

Help!

How could I have gotten myself into such a terrible mess! There was no escape from the depression that had hit a low beyond anything I had experienced. I was drowning!

I had been so pleased when I arrived at their home in the middle of the country, a place I had visited on numerous occasions with Paul, and received a heartwarming reception from Chris and Heidi. In looking around the farm, I saw a combination of rare and exotic plants as well as a few small and friendly barnyard animals; I knew that there would be plenty of work to occupy my every waking moment. I could be kept busy for as long as I wanted and staying busy was really what I wanted.....or thought I wanted.

Paul and I had met Chris in the first year of our world travels. He was a bearded giant of a man wearing size fifteen shoes with a pleasant smile and a soft Dutch accent. He was vacationing in the Canary Islands while Heidi had gone to visit her family in Austria. He wasn't enjoying his vacation until we came along and invited him to join us in seeing some of the sights. We rented a car and since he was too long-legged to sit in the front seat he had the entire back seat to himself and could unfold his lanky body sideways to some degree.

"You'll have to come to England to meet my Heidi," he would say often, and on one of our return trips to England we did meet her. She was just as Chris had described – petite, blond, and very energetic. She was a lot of fun, with a head filled with exciting ideas, plans, jokes and stories. She was an unpublished writer of children's books and had frequently told us her stories, each character using a different voice. She was a

Digging In

gourmet cook who loved to experiment with the various ingredients that she found in the garden, and I never once saw her use a cookbook. Unfortunately, she washed everything only as thoroughly as she felt necessary and assured us that 'the good earth' was as valuable inside as outside. At every meal there was something in there that either rattled every tooth in our head when we crunched down or ground down our molars with a not-so-fine sand that needed a little more spray before going down the drain. Most of her meals were incredibly tasty because she instinctually seemed to know what ingredients went well together. She never apologized for what we felt shouldn't have been in there in the first place. To add to her charm she was a holistic medical healer and a bit of the devil all rolled into one. Paul and I loved her from the moment we met her.

I was thrilled when she had told me to come to The Garden of Eden Center and assured me that there would be lots of work to do. Physical labor seemed to help control my mental anguish. I thought that if I wore myself down physically I would not think too much. Since I never slept well anyway I looked forward to absolute exhaustion.

I spent the day after my arrival with Chris. We were selling plants at a flower show in the local county fair. It would have been more interesting had we been busier but it was a start. Much of the time I was left alone and when Chris came back to relieve me I wandered around the show. The plants, mostly weed-like, all started to look the same by the end of the day and I was glad to get back to The Center and to some interesting conversation. That day Heidi caught up on paperwork and shipping.

The next day I was propagating plants after a few minutes of instructions. The job required the shoving and lifting of boxes of large plants with tons of earth to weigh them down. Each plant was in its own plastic pot in the box. The

Chasing the Lost Dream

plant had to be removed from the pot, leaving behind most of the somewhat dry earth and then ripped apart by hand. Each half of the plant along with some of the root system and fresh earth was re-potted into a smaller pot and put aside in a large tray along with others in their family grouping. I swear that by the end of the day I was re-potting weeds that looked exactly like something rare and exotic.

Heidi kept me company for brief periods of time, always approaching with something cold to drink or a piece of cut fruit to nibble on, and only occasionally checking the work. She thanked me for being there almost every time she saw me. She also guaranteed me that they were all real plants that would eventually be sold as opposed to something that would be sprayed, removed and burned.

It was a tedious job and I disliked it because I was alone much of the time. Heidi had lots of her own work to do in various parts of the garden, and Chris was always somewhere in the garden but practically invisible to the naked eye. How someone that enormous could blend in that well simply amazed me.

The physical labor eased my distraught mind but the work was far too taxing on my unfit body. I ignored the early warning signs, thinking that I would get used to it. Within three days I had done such heavy, constant lifting and shoving around of those flat-tray boxes that I pulled my back out and dared not straighten up.

With every move I was in agony, so I took a day off to sit with pillows propping up my back. I used a variety of painkillers, both pill-form and rub-form, to relieve the soreness while I read *Pillars of the Earth* by Ken Follett. When I got too bleary-eyed to read I watched a few of my favorite comedy television shows. For that day the work continued without me and I tried not to feel guilty about lying there on the couch. The

Digging In

next day was worse. Much, much worse. I couldn't even get out of bed.

Heidi served me breakfast in bed and brought a little bell to my night stand. "Just ring it and I'll come running," she said with a little smile, and promptly left to attend the plants in the greenhouse at the bottom of the garden. She would not have heard Big Ben chiming out the noon bells from that distance.

By the third day I was walking around slowly, hunched over and holding onto my aching sides like they would split apart if I let go. Despite the fact that I had never been on a computer Heidi decided to teach me a few games. It didn't take long to learn the games, and for her to teach me to update her address files. I seemed to be in my element. Only the computer was new to me; typing was something I did really well and I had no problems reading the orders and addresses.

It was while sitting in the office, talking quietly, that she confided to me how unhappy she was with all the work that had to be done. Besides much of the heavy labor, which Chris loved but couldn't do by himself, she handled all the bookkeeping, all the computer work, all the shipping, all the packaging, all the housework, all the cooking and all the animal feeding. Her body and her spirit were having trouble coping with working non-stop. Arthritis was also taking its toll. She desperately wanted "out."

From the moment she confessed her unhappiness she talked about it incessantly. From the moment she confessed her unhappiness I withdrew into my own unhappy little world. I struggled with my depression in silence. With every bit of conversation I wondered why my husband had been taken while hers just hung around as an annoyance. The tension soon became unbearable.

One day, after a morning of work, Heidi and I played games on the computer. Chris pushed the door open, and in a

Chasing the Lost Dream

voice that would wake the dead, boomed, "LUNCH." No prelude, no niceties, just LUNCH. I actually thought he must be kidding but his voice scared the hell out of me. Looking at her wristwatch Heidi said that it was past his lunch time and that lunch should be on the table. Lunch, I was told, was to be served at one in the afternoon. It was now three minutes past one and he was furious.

After that incident my mood turned black. I knew that I had to get away. I knew also that I had no idea where I would be going. I still had some friends that I wanted to visit but I felt I could not leave immediately without Heidi knowing why and I'm not sure why I cared, but I did. I had also promised both of them that I would work a major county show and fair in Peterborough.

I slumped into a dangerous depression and had no one to talk to about it. Heidi saw the change in me immediately and knew, for the most part, that she had been the cause.

We didn't talk much about personal things after that. She gave me a variety of jobs to do that were not the least bit taxing on my body, and in much more of a familiar element: I typed labels. I addressed and stuffed envelopes. I made up bank deposits and checked figures, all of which I had done in my own business and in the numerous offices where I had worked during my various careers.

We spent a day at the health club doing water aerobics, floor exercises and swimming. We talked about the upcoming county fair that we would be attending. So the days passed.....

I was excited as we drove to the Peterborough Show and Fair. Heidi rode with me and Chris drove his truck with one of his employees as a passenger, pulling a trailer stocked with thousands of plants stacked from floor to ceiling. After the men set up the display Heidi and I had three days of working by

Digging In

ourselves. Chris went off to exhibit and sell at another flower show in London.

It was absolutely amazing how relaxed everything got without him around. We could work, talk, enjoy the customers, and drown ourselves in a sea of coffee and soft drinks. Business was brisk and constant. We ate when we were hungry and took breaks when we could.

Since Heidi had been doing the Peterborough show for many years by herself most of the customers knew and loved her. She made sure that I was introduced to everyone, and she seemed to know every customer by name as well as the plants that they had purchased in past years. One customer invited us back to his home for dinner and we gratefully accepted. After the show closed for the evening our host, Bob Thomas, came to pick us up.

That evening there was lots of pleasant conversation, a wine jug that was never empty, and easy-going laughter from the simplest of jokes along with a tour of the beautiful gardens that surrounded the house. Most of the exotic plants had been purchased from The Garden of Eden Center and each one had a special place in the garden and in their hearts.

It didn't take me long to tire of listening to stories about the plants, since I had been with the plants much longer than I wanted to be. I much preferred a tour of the house, with it's large, country-style kitchen and enormous dining room. The living room was made for relaxing and chatting, and was decorated in an easy-on-the-eyes hunter green. That evening was the highlight of the show, and thankfully I regained much of my humor.

On the last day of the show Chris returned with Jimmy, his employee, to pack up. Jimmy drove with me and I was grateful for the company. Since I would not have been able to follow Chris in the dark I was relieved to have someone with

Chasing the Lost Dream

me who knew the way home. He had a soft Jamaican accent but didn't talk much, except to tell me about some of the quirky customers at the London show.

We met up with Heidi and Chris at a favorite restaurant for dinner about halfway through our trip. Once back at the house things quickly turned unbearably ugly again. It was not what they were saying - it was what they weren't saying. I could feel the tension. It was steaming and bubbling like red-hot lava was right under the surface. I didn't want to be around when it exploded a mile high in the air. I knew that it would.

I tried to keep my distance but it did not work. While at The Center I wrote some letters back to my friends and family in Canada and they all worried about me for weeks. The depression poured out of my heart right onto the paper and I couldn't stop it. There was no one at the nursery that I could talk to and it was killing me.

I needed out!

Chapter 15

More Friends

I had been at The Garden of Eden Center, and I use that particular term very loosely, for over two weeks when I called my friend Andrea in Otford to ask if the proposed archaeological dig had started in Sevenoaks. I felt the dig would be a perfect excuse to leave without causing any bad feelings, and I still had no idea why I felt it was important not to cause any bad feelings. Andrea answered "no, not yet. Are you all right?"

"I'll be okay," I replied.

Without a word of explanation, just the sound of my voice, my friend sensed that I was not all right. I got off the phone and decided that if I didn't make the break I would surely go insane. I had a pocketful of coins and with my little black phone book handy I placed another call. This one was to Brian and Ellen Nix, living only thirty miles away in Creeting St. Mary. I tried not to let my desperation ruin a pleasant phone conversation.

When Ellen extended an open invitation I felt an instant relief and told her I would be on my way in the next day or two. I breathed a little easier on the way back to the nursery. I walked a little straighter and a little faster, with that spring in my step that only comes from a light heart. My shoulders relaxed.

I stayed at the exotic plant nursery one more day and vowed that I would never put myself in such an uncomfortable position again. I didn't have to say too much to Heidi. She knew. The tension in the house was no less for her, only more familiar.

Chasing the Lost Dream

We said our good-byes after breakfast the next morning knowing that we probably would never see each other again. With each mile of the drive to Creeting St. Mary my confidence peeked out a little further from under the heavy black cloud of doom and gloom. Despite some trouble finding the house, since I was sure that Longacres, the name of their cottage, would be on a sign on the mailbox, I didn't get flustered. When I didn't find their name or the name of the cottage I stopped to peer around every out-of-the-way driveway to see if I could spot their motorhome. I recognized it immediately behind a hedge of tall bushes.

Brian and Ellen came out when they heard my camper pull onto their driveway - they had been waiting for me. I got a warm hug from both and Ellen broke free to walk around the van.

"Isn't Paul with you?" she asked, her eyes wide open, waiting for an answer to the question she thought was silly.

Paul and I had met the Nix's while camping at a campground right across the street from a beach on the Costa Del Sol in Spain. They had been part of a large group from England that had befriended us. Brian and Ellen were warm, welcoming people whose playful bickering was from a long-standing and loving marriage. They were absolutely stunned to hear that Paul had died over a year before, and were even more shocked at what I was doing.....traveling around in a foreign country by myself.

I tried putting the events of the last few weeks behind me so I could enjoy their company. I spent my days helping out with the gardening.....nothing backbreaking or mind numbing like my experience at The Garden.....just a pleasant amount of exercise out in the sunshine. Brian showed me how to use the electric trimmer and I flattened out one section of the hedge that ran around their huge back yard. It wasn't quite as even as it

Digging In

could have been but I was assured that "it'll grow back." I mowed a good piece of their acreage with a hand mower, something I was familiar with from years gone by at our home in Beeton, Ontario, about 50 miles north of Toronto.

They had a greenhouse where they were growing cacti that would spend their entire lives in the warm, dry confines of the arboretum, several of them large enough to take up residency and fit in perfectly in an Arizona saguaro field.

We enjoyed a couple of pub lunches. We visited local gardens and hothouses where they could check out the latest in plants, the newest garden magazines, or pick up the latest seed catalogue, something that only vaguely interested me. I was just along for the ride....

We spent one afternoon visiting Great Yarmouth, home of the largest motorhome dealership in England. Since we were all familiar with living in a motorhome this was a real event for all of us. Although the dealership was only a couple of hours drive from their home they turned it into a whole day's affair, picnic and all. We viewed several new motorhomes, most of them small enough for me to handle alone, if I chose to, but costing more money than I ever would have spent. There was even a used one; a Coachmen that had been left behind for sale by an American couple who had been touring England and the continent for a year. It definitely had seen better days. The padding in the seats was lumpy. The wallpaper was dirty and peeling in spots. The kitchen area needed a good scrubbing and I wondered if everything, or anything for that matter, worked, but the steering wheel was on the left side, where it is supposed to be, and I suddenly felt very nostalgic until I saw the price tag and choked. I could have purchased a new one, right off the assembly line with a bumper-to-bumper warranty, for less than they wanted for this one. We talked about it all the way home.

Chasing the Lost Dream

While going through Ipswich on the way home I found myself needing some cash. I used my new bank card for the first time. The ATM machine spit money back at me so fast I hardly had time to get my hands under it. The machine wanted my secret access code and the amount. It did not care what bank, whether it was a savings or checking account, or what country the money came from. It just spewed out beautifully colored, Queen decorated, paper money in ten and twenty-pound notes. I now felt a little more secure, knowing that my traveling money was as close as any ATM.

We discussed my life during another of our pub lunches, and although I could see the sadness in her eyes, probably reflected from my own, Ellen issued a challenge. She took me to the travel section of her favorite bookstore and told me she expected to see my name amongst the authors on that shelf within five years. This was a real challenge because I was not writing at the time.....nor had I ever seriously considered writing.

My friends seemed so proud of my accomplishments. Ellen was sure that my spunk would lead to a different type of life.....and a good one.

The three days went by very quickly with only one incident that damn near drove me over the edge of sanity. That would not have been a long trip since my recent return from the brink of hell.

The night before my departure, while watching television, I spotted a gargantuan creature affixed about halfway down the opposite wall. Spider was not exactly the word I would have used to describe it. When this monstrosity started walking I could feel the vibration where I sat. It not only had a plethora of long, thick legs like it had been working out on a Thigh Master since spidyhood, it had an enormous, dark, round body. I wasn't close enough to see if the body was covered with

Digging In

hair or fur or feathers but that wasn't important. My eyes were glued to the sight of the thing. I could not yell. I could only point, wild-eyed and frantic. Ellen followed my gaze and when her eyes settled on the monster she screamed for Brian. I'm sure she screamed just to humor me.

I was absolutely terrified. Except for seeing tarantulas behind a wall of glass inside an aquarium at the pet shop, I had never seen any insect so big and with so many thick, muscular legs.

Brian sauntered into the room, looked around and without a word went back into the kitchen. He returned quickly with a four-quart, wide-mouthed jar and a newspaper in hand. He gently ushered the spider into the jar, covered the mouth of the jar with the newspaper and left the house via the back door. He was gone so long that when he returned Ellen asked sarcastically: "What did you do, take it to the pub for a drink? Where the heck did you go?"

In his usual soft-spoken manner he explained that spiders have a homing device and if released too close to the house they will turn around and march, goose-step style, right back into the house. I took it out to the orchard and put it in a tree," he explained.

"Wonderful," I repeated a couple of times, "a homing device." With visions of spiders dangling by a fragile web descending from the ceiling, I hardly slept that night and insisted that the light be left on. Over breakfast we talked and said our good-byes. I assured them that I would return before going back to Canada. I hugged and thanked them. It had been these few days that had renewed my faith in myself.

I was becoming more and more used to it; however, up to this point I really had not spent much time sleeping or camping in the van and I really needed to do this.

Chasing the Lost Dream

Each time I got behind the steering wheel I felt like a pioneer!

Chapter 16

On the Coast

I felt guilty. Deep down I knew that I should be spending more time on my own just to see if I could handle it, but I couldn't stand more than a few minutes of my life by myself. I needed to be with someone......anyone.

Every time I felt that I was letting my friends do too much for me I was reminded of the wise words of Sister Jean DeVita, head of the bereavement group that I had attended in Toronto right after Paul's death. "If anyone wants to help you, let them. You will have time to repay them, or someone else, when you are stronger." As much as I hated imposing on everyone I let her kind words guide me. I called friends in Norwich, that guilty feeling pushed to the back of my mind once more, when Dave answered the phone.

Dee and Dave Hunt, whom Paul and I had met in Athens, Greece, invited me to their home. As a group of six, with Amy and Norman Prestup from New Jersey, we had spent several months together touring the Greek Islands. They had heard about Paul from the Prestups and they wanted to see for themselves that I was okay. When I called from Creeting St. Mary Dave, with Dee muttering in the background, gave me directions to Norwich and I was to call when I was close to the city. I had their address handy because I had written to them on several occasions but they were shocked when they opened the door on the first knock and found me on their doorstep. Like my friends in Temple Cloud on the other side of the country, Dave was sure he would have to come retrieve me from some back alley in Norwich after a pathetic call for help. British maps, I was delighted to discover, were very precise and even

Chasing the Lost Dream

the tiniest off-the-beaten-track road was marked with a street name and a route number.

After a couple of quick hugs, the yakking started even before the tea was made and we whiled away the afternoon and a good part of the evening bringing each other up-to-date on the current events in our lives.

Dee and Dave were younger than all the other travelers that Paul and I had befriended on our two-and-a-half year adventure, so there was a lot of talk about work and jobs and the lack thereof. Although Dee worked in the medical field and always managed to find work, Dave worked in sales in department stores and was constantly having to change jobs as money became tighter and things slowed down. He would occasionally hire himself out for police lineups when money was short.

Their apartment was tiny but I was told that the living room, with a very comfortable sleeper sofa, was all mine for as long as I wanted to stay.

As of the next day they were both on vacation. Their one vacation chore was to repaint their bedroom with a paint that would inhibit mold. It was a problem that many English homes and apartments had – the place was damp.

"I'll stay," I said, "but only if I can help. With the three of us working full tilt we could finish in record time and have time for some sightseeing." They readily agreed.

The first day was spent stripping the existing wallpaper. By the end of that day Dee and Dave were at each other's throats, and I worried that I would lose the comforts of the couch if it was relegated to Dave. He was vanquished from the bedroom and assigned to removing some of the rust spots on my van. I worked with Dee. The various jobs went very smoothly after that. We worked and talked and ate and cried for about five days, stopping only for meals and nightfall. I loved

68

Digging In

the physical labor. After several coats of the heavy, goopy-style paint and a couple of coats of off-white we could see the marvelous results.

Dave was thrilled with the bedroom and I was thrilled when I saw the job that he had done on the van. Every spot removed made the van a little more marketable. He removed all of them, even the one with the dent that Paul got sideswiping a metal pole divider while trying to back out of a parking spot at a supermarket in Albir, Spain.

Lunches were a grab and run sandwich affair but dinners were planned and well thought out. Dee prepared vegetarian bean and rice delights while I supplied a bottle of wine for the occasion. On alternate evenings I paid for dinners out. At home Dave was a vegetarian like Dee because she refused to have meat cooking indoors. Out of the house he was a carnivore like me. Food-wise, the days and nights were absolutely delicious.

While watching the news on television one evening we learned that an archaeological dig was underway and objects "of major importance" were found in Scole, thirteen miles inland.

I was up around dawn and out the door right after breakfast the next morning. With easy to follow directions, I went to the museum in Norwich to volunteer my services at the dig. I filled out an application and returned home very excited about my prospects. I waited.....and waited.....and waited for the telephone call that never came.

Almost two weeks passed.

Chapter 17

Success.....Finally

The days had gone by much too fast! As much as she hated to see it happen, Dee went back to work. Dave put the finishing touches on my van and was preparing to go back to work in a day or two. Although we had not spent our days sitting idly around the apartment, I had not heard from the museum and was not looking forward to spending my days alone wandering around an empty three-room flat or trying to find things to occupy my time in and around Norwich.

"Do you want to take a ride out to Scole tomorrow and see what's happening at the dig?" I asked Dave.

His eyes popped open immediately and glowed with anticipation. A slow, wide grin spread across his face. He wholeheartedly agreed; thought the idea was "smashing."

Right after breakfast the next morning, we drove the thirteen miles on the main road out of the city in their tiny, brilliantly white, spotlessly clean and totally rust-free Cooper Mini. This was my first time riding in the front seat. When Dee was with us I had to fold and unfold myself from the back seat.....what there was of it anyway. I didn't feel the least bit safe in it when I could actually SEE how big the other cars were coming at us compared to the sardine can we were riding around in. Fortunately we weren't going a long distance and I could squeeze my eyelids shut when I got really scared, which was during most of the drive.

We had no trouble finding the dig site. It was enormous and clearly visible from the main road going through the town. We took the closest exit and were at the gates within minutes.

Digging In

There were many people milling around the small building, located right inside the open gate.

Dave and I watched some of the goings-on from behind the fencing. There were several people down on their hands and knees in the field and their noses were so close to the dirt that I expected to see a little mound of earth sitting on top of their proboscis when they looked up. Others, dressed like the rest of the group in the field, waited in the doorway of the one-storey building. Still others stood around talking to each other, seemingly not paying attention to anything but their own conversation.

When the entire group had left the office I walked in and asked to speak to the person in charge. A pleasant-looking young woman asked if she could help. I screwed up my courage and asked if they needed any volunteers, my voice suddenly taking on a quiver that wasn't there ten minutes earlier.

"When did you have your last tetanus shot?" asked Alice Landis.

I answered "September 1989."

"When would you like to start?" she asked.

Dave, who waited behind the fence and had been watching the slow, meticulous work going on in the field, could tell by my smile that all had gone well. "So much for waiting by the phone for the museum to call," I quipped. "Could we drive around a bit and find a campground?" I asked.

We continued on down the main road. The drive to the closest campground was less than a mile and the only thing separating the campground from the dig was a creek with a couple of inches of slow moving water. We drove up the lane to the two-storey brick house and could see a few campers parked behind the house.

Chasing the Lost Dream

"I don't want to be driving back and forth every day and I really think that it's time I was on my own," I said to Dave.

After a couple of knuckle-crunching knocks an elderly, chubby, white-haired woman answered the door. I told her that I needed a camping spot for a couple of weeks because I would be working at the dig. Without a moment's hesitation she said, "No, I'm sorry. We used to let people from the dig in here but they were too dirty and they messed up our bathrooms. They never cleaned up after themselves. They were too loud. You can't stay here," she said emphatically and tried to close the door.

"Please," I said, "I'm alone and I need a safe place to stay and camp. I won't be doing any of the digging so I won't be getting your showers all dirty. I'm visiting here from Canada for the summer. Please," I said. "Please don't turn me away." If it sounds like I was begging, it's because I was begging.

After much pleading and guaranteeing that I would be quiet and clean and willing to follow any orders she gave, she finally relented.

* * * *

We stopped at the grocery store on the way home. That night we had an extra special bottle of bubbly wine with dinner to celebrate. Both Dee and Dave said that they didn't mind if I stayed in the campground during the week but they wanted me at their place for the weekends. "Besides," said Dave "we want to hear, first hand, what's going on at the dig. We want the news before the telly gets it," he grinned.

I had one last day off to prepare. I cleaned out the inside of the van since I hadn't been in it the whole time I was with the Hunts. I washed the windows, turned on the refrigerator and

Digging In

loaded it with perishables, and put the cans in the cupboards. I re-packed most of my washed and folded clothes into one of the bench seats of the camper. I was actually humming out loud the whole time I was packing. I was all set to go and really excited.

I cooked a vegetarian spaghetti dinner for the three of us that we washed down with a glass and a half of stuff that actually tickled my nose. By seven dinner was over, the dishes were washed and put away, and our comfy clothes were changed for something a little more appropriate for a special occasion. We walked the few blocks to the Norwich Cathedral for a Pre-Tour Concert by the Norwich Cathedral Choir and a stroll around the rather sparse-looking grounds. The music was not exactly to my liking but I enjoyed the evening out and the walk to and from the apartment, along with meeting some of Dee and Dave's friends and neighbors.

We were home after eleven and since the following day was a workday for everyone we went right to bed. I tossed and turned and checked the clock glowing at my bedside every couple of hours through the night.

It was a long night!

Chapter 18

A Member of the Group

The excitement of finally having something that I considered 'important' to do with my life could not be contained. I was out of bed before the sun. I left the apartment so early and the drive had been so easy that I arrived before the crew and anyone looking like they might be in charge. The building used as an office was locked.

I was sitting on a bench looking down at the site and daydreaming for more than a quarter of an hour when three mini vans followed each other into the compound and stopped in front of the hut. The crew, nine in each van, exited like bees erupting from the hive.

The crew members picked up their assignments. When I approached Alice, now known to me as the crew chief, she asked if I wouldn't mind waiting until after the briefing. I made myself a pot of tea, then sat and fidgeted in my van, anxiously awaiting my 'official' orders.

Once everyone else was at work it took her no time at all to find an assignment for me. By the time I was ready to go to work there were seven other volunteers that had shown up. We sat in our own little room at a large table with plastic bags full of 'findings' in front of us. We introduced ourselves. I was the only foreigner in the bunch and the only one who had come from more than a walking distance away. The others seemed to all know each other and were either friends or neighbors before the dig, or they had worked together long enough to be comfortable with each other. When we took a tea and biscuit break we chitchatted but even then it was only about the dig. Nothing personal ever made it into the conversation.

Digging In

We all did the same job. The center of the large, wooden, rectangular table that we worked at was heaped with small, clear plastic bags. We each took a bag, and emptied it directly in front of us. Besides the findings, there was a piece of paper, no larger than one-inch square, in the bag with the grid number on it along with the name of the site.

With a nib pen, taken from the batch in the center of the table, and India ink I started marking each piece, no matter how small, with the bag number and a large 'S' for the dig site, 'Scole.' Despite the tedium of the job and the lack of conversation, the workday was over much too quickly.

The first day at the dig did not prepare me for my first night at the campground alone. It was my first night alone in the camper since those awful days in Cardiff. I busied myself preparing dinner on my two-burner stove like I had done so often when I traveled with Paul. I also pulled a good novel out of the large pile of books that I had to read and left it sitting on the bench seat.

After dinner and dish washing, drying and putting everything where it belonged in the cupboard, knowing that I had all evening to myself, I could feel the wind being knocked out of my sails. I could feel depression coming up from my depths. While it was still light and before settling down, I walked through the campground studying the few camping vans that were there. One camper was the exact size as the one I had been looking at in Great Yarmouth. However, since it was still around dinnertime, I did not disturb the occupants.

I watched from my van; when the man left the camper carrying the dinner dishes and a pot I quickly went over and knocked on the door. It was a pleasant-looking older woman who answered. With whatever smile I could muster I explained that I had been looking at this exact same camper and asked

Chasing the Lost Dream

"how do you like this size of van?" She promptly invited me in and gave me the cook's tour.

I was getting ready to leave when her husband returned. He opened the door, saw me standing there, and said rather exuberantly: "How wonderful! We have a guest. Let's have tea."

We talked about their travels around England and bits of France, all places that I had been to with Paul. They listened eagerly about my extensive travels through Europe and parts of Africa, and reveled in my travels through my homelands of Canada and the United States. They were intrigued by the stories about the dig and the people who were working there. I touched only briefly on why I was traveling alone and changed the subject quickly so I wouldn't break down into tears, since my bottom lip was already starting to quiver.

Long past bedtime, flashlight in hand, Peter and Jean walked me back to my camper and made sure that all was well before they left me. I was tired from my workday, relieved that the long evening had passed so pleasantly, and was ready for a good night's sleep. I set my alarm for eight but was up long before it went off. Their Swift camper was gone before I went to work the next morning.

The dig became a lot more interesting and personally satisfying the next day. Andy, a group leader, gave all the volunteers an in-depth tour of the site. He explained that many of the larger and more interesting pieces that had been unearthed had already been transferred to the museum in Norwich; however, they had recently dug up a sarcophagus, complete with body inside, and were working on removing it. We gathered round as he pointed out some fascinating details.

"The coffin is small and built with a double thickness lid that has collapsed in on itself," he explained. "We are not yet certain if it is the body of a child or if the person buried is

Digging In

doubled over. If it is a child it will be a royal child because children are usually buried out in the field, not in double caskets."

Other graves had also been found, along with lots of pottery shards. The pottery was taken to the volunteer area, where our group would soon be in the process of numbering all the day's pieces. Again day's end came far too quickly and the one-mile drive was far too short.

My dinners were hot, simple and fast. My desire to make imaginative, flavorful and colorful meals died with Paul. I ate as slowly as I possibly could, just to kill some time. While washing the dishes in the sink in the ladies room, I chatted with a young woman. She was delighted with the fact that it was so quiet and peaceful in the campground.

"I'm alone," I said trying to keep the conversation light, "so I wish there were more people around."

Dishes done and not being able to think of anything else to say, I said goodnight and wandered back to my camper. I was there only a few minutes when there was a knock at the door.

"If you don't want to be by yourself," said the young woman, "please join us at our tent. We have two children and they are asleep so we can't leave."

I needed no coaxing. I put on my sneakers and was lacing them up before she even finished the sentence. I picked up a bottle of wine from my storage area under the stove, grabbed my sweatshirt that had been neatly folded and shoved into the compartment under the seat, and was off before she could change her mind.

John and Margaret were both in their late twenties or early thirties. Their children, whom I didn't see nor hear, were three and five, and slept through our talking and story-telling, not even waking when we laughed a bit too loud. When the

Chasing the Lost Dream

wine was gone they made a pot of tea, and when that was gone it was time to call it a night. While Margaret checked on the children, John walked me back to my camper.

I don't know how long I tossed and turned but I finally took a sleeping pill and fell asleep.

The next day was another fascinating one. A complete body was found, and as decayed as it was, the brain remained intact. Janis, one of the other volunteers decided that the newspaper headlines should read, "Finally Someone in Norfolk with Brains." We all howled at the suggestion.

I made the comment that since the body had a brain "it must be a woman," and one of the guys shot back immediately: "Yes, it's a woman; we could tell by the well-developed lower jaw from talking too much." There were many jokes going around and in the end it was determined that it was a woman because she was wearing jewelry.

The workday ended early. That afternoon I drove back to Norwich for the weekend. Dinner was a lively one as I told Dee and Dave what was going on at the dig. They were absolutely fascinated because the news from the dig was being shown on the television every day at six o'clock, but this time they were hearing about stuff that the newscasters did not report. They loved the details and with so many questions to ask the conversation didn't end until bedtime.

We spent Saturday shopping. I took some money out of my account with an ATM card, the process of which still had me fascinated. At the second-hand bookstore I traded a few that I had read and some that I just couldn't get into. I purchased some stamps and mailed letters back to family and friends in Canada.

On Sunday our early morning seven-mile walk was canceled because of rain. By the time afternoon rolled around the sun was out. We went to the market town of Beccles to

Digging In

check out the new and used wares at each booth. When one of the hot dog vendors found out I lived in Florida he offered to become my boy toy.

"How old are you?" asked Dee.

"I'm thirty-eight," he answered.

"You're too old for my friend," she answered even though I was close to fifty. "I don't want anyone over thirty-five for her. I want someone young enough so that you're changing her diaper and not the other way around."

We walked away giggling and left the poor hot dog vendor scratching and shaking his head as he put our money in his cash register. Dave and I had well-roasted hot dogs with mustard dripping out the bottom of the bun, while Dee was nibbling on some greasy chips.

Before the day was over we drove out to Great Yarmouth to see some motorhomes. I was getting a really good idea of what I wanted the next time around!

Chapter 19

Stoneleigh Festival

The second week of volunteering at the dig flew by just as quickly as the first. My primary job continued to be the same as all other volunteers, which was putting numbers and locations on each artifact, no matter how small or seemingly insignificant. For the most part it was okay. A very special camaraderie had developed amongst us and I was enjoying the light-heartedness of it all and the banter that came along with it.

When I couldn't straighten up from hunching over the daily finds and really needed a change of pace, they had me scrubbing the recent findings with a toothbrush and finger-numbing ice water. Where they found that much bone-chilling water, since what came out of the tap was closer in temperature to pee, or why they couldn't dribble a thimbleful of warm water into the pan, I'll never know. It was perhaps why I was the only one who volunteered for scrubbing duty. Obviously my colleagues knew better.

By the second week a couple of the other volunteers found out about my situation and one after another they took me home for the evening and drove me back to the campground and the security of my camper long after dark. The invitations started with John, the only man working in the group, who invited me to his home at the special request of his wife, Maggie. They were a charming older couple, who looked very much like Jack Spratt who could eat no fat with a wife who could eat no lean. Dinner, which was put on the table the minute we came through the front door and seconds after I was introduced, was a simple affair with bowls full of cooked carrots and peas and beans, boiled potatoes and a minuscule

Digging In

amount of meat. There was a large loaf of homemade bread in the center of the table still warm from the oven that, I was told, "could be sliced thick or thin or torn apart with fingers." With an extended hand I was told simply to "dig in." While Maggie grabbed the peas, John grabbed the carrots and each bowl was passed around the table. No one went hungry. The homemade, still piping hot, apple pie with a pot of tea at the end of the meal was heartwarmingly delicious.

John and Maggie were eager to hear about my travels and marveled at my gumption of doing it alone. Neither had traveled beyond England so they peppered me with questions and listened eagerly for the long, sometimes involved, answers. We talked well past midnight and I was grateful that I didn't have to drive home alone in the dark, even though during daylight hours would have been only a short walk.

The situation I forced on myself would have been intolerable had it not been for the wonderful people, many of whose names I have forgotten or never knew, that I met along the way.

*　　*　　*　　*

Even though none of the jobs were overly interesting and all the work was slow and meticulous, which I wasn't used to, there was an unmistakable friendship amongst everyone in our little room.....regular or temporary staff and volunteers. Everyone was there for a reason, whether it was a job for money or a chance to be part of uncovering ancient history, or as in my case, just to forget my own personal sadness for a little while and be a participant in life.

By the end of that next week I realized that I had not spent one evening alone and that suited me just fine. I returned to Dee and Dave's place on the weekend one last time and was

Chasing the Lost Dream

welcomed like a conquering hero. Within minutes I was able to tell them about all the television and newspaper crews that had been hanging about and we turned on the evening news to see the happenings at the dig site. We were more than halfway through the allotted dig time and it was determined that the Scole dig was the most significant find of the year. It was so exciting just to be there, but for me it was rapidly coming to a close.

When the need for volunteers diminished I prepared to leave and was presented with a triangular shard of Samien Pottery, about two inches wide at the base, three inches tall that came to a pointy top. It was found outside of the dig boundaries and given as souvenirs to school children and special guests. I was thanked profusely by Alice and the few crew members that I got to know and by the volunteers. I was told that I would be welcomed back anytime at any of the Norwich dig sites.

It was early on a Wednesday morning that I went back to the home of Brian and Ellen Nix in Creeting St. Mary. They were delighted that I had decided to follow them to a camping festival in Stoneleigh. We had only the one day to prepare for the trip. Fortunately, in between working and socializing and generally running around, I had done a couple of loads of laundry at the campground so my clothes were clean, folded and neatly packed under the seat. We did some grocery shopping before we left, and were on the road early Thursday morning.

As grateful as I was to be included, by the time we arrived in Stoneleigh I was ready to murder them both. It seems that they had decided to take the scenic route rather than the straight, open highway from point A (Creeting St. Mary) to point B (Stoneleigh). We drove at least three extra hours through all the small towns and villages with my left hand shifting from first to second and occasionally to third, but never long enough to give my hand and arm a rest. Every hundred

Digging In

yards there was another damn stop signal and I had no one to scream at. What a pain in the ass!

It was only when we stopped for lunch that I was asked how I was enjoying the gorgeous scenery, none of which I saw because I was too busy not running up their tailpipe. I gave my report through gritted teeth that were sore from the workout. We never did get on a highway because at that point we were too far away from one. Thankfully they drove a little quicker, making sure that I stayed within spitting distance in their rear view mirror.

I was deliriously happy when we arrived at the festival. Although I had been seeing giant hot air balloons flying as I approached, I was not aware that it was that kind of festival. They were gorgeous, and when one of them accidentally came down near the parked campers everyone went running over there. "Make them pay the entrance fee. They are trying to sneak in without paying," some of the campers shouted. After making sure the balloonists were okay we had a good laugh.

The weekend was both healing and profitable. I camped with approximately four hundred other campers. There were morning tea-and-crumpet get-togethers. There were mid-day or evening parties to attend. There were people I had met years earlier while camping in Spain with Paul, so I did a bit of reminiscing.

I took the opportunity, with so many campers around, to sell off my excess: the battery-operated radio we had purchased in Gibraltar, Paul's golf clubs and bag, the round, heavy plastic table and two deck chairs. I put a sign in the window to sell the van. People seemed interested and asked a lot of questions, but in the end there were no buyers.

After the rally in Stoneleigh I said goodbye to Brian and Ellen and made my way back to Otford and my Canadian friends via the highways. Andrea had a little pile of envelopes

Chasing the Lost Dream

for me. There were several letters from my sister and one from each of my brothers. A few letters came from friends. One was a birthday party invitation from dear, sweet Marjorie Jones.

Paul and I had met Marjorie and her husband Don while camping in France. She was one of my favorite people on our two-and-a-half year journey, from the instant we met. On our first meeting they confessed their ages and the fact that they had been married less than a month. Over the years we maintained a close friendship by visiting them in Spain several times and with letters and postcards going back and forth across "the pond" several times a year.

I called Marjorie's son, Neil Roche, whom I had met several times, immediately upon opening the invitation. I informed him that I would be there "with bells on."

Marjorie would be turning seventy. She was as charming, as warm and as entertaining a woman as Paul and I had ever met. Don was an American from California and we occasionally let him know that we loved him in spite of that flaw. Marjorie was Welsh.

I would not have missed Marjorie's party and an opportunity to see them both again under any circumstances. The party would take place in three weeks and I was determined to stay busy until that time.

Chapter 20

One Last Dig.....One Last Party

I made myself comfortable one last time in Otford. I stayed to help Andrea who was six months pregnant and exhausted most of the time. Cooking and caring for two very rambunctious boys had become rather overwhelming to her.

I enjoyed being back in a house, doing ordinary chores. I cooked dinner every night; I folded the mountain of laundry after it was line-dried. And at the end of every evening, after the dishes had been loaded into the machine ready to go, I flopped down in front of the television set and vegged out. That was the way I spent almost every night.

During the day, however, I had the opportunity of working on one last archaeological dig that had recently begun. I drove to Sevenoaks and signed up as a volunteer. When my application heralded the fact that I had participated in two previous digs they were delighted and anxious to have me come on board.

The dig was taking place in St. Bartholomew's Church, about a ten-mile drive from my temporary residence in Otford. The reason for the dig was explained: "In the eleventh century Sevenoaks became a market town and the church had expanded in all four directions to accommodate all the new people coming to town. When the townsfolk died they paid a premium to be buried in the church basement. The last burial took place around nineteen hundred. This particular dig is to find the original walls of the church and to remove all the bodies and rebury them in the churchyard. After the dig is completed they will be building a tearoom in the basement."

Chasing the Lost Dream

The basement was damp. Most of the flooring had been dug up long before I arrived, leaving the raw ground exposed and smelling 'earthy.' It was not unpleasant but unless I was moving around or working I needed to see that it was light outside.

Several rooms in the basement had been cordoned off for meetings. The larger meeting room had file drawers and papers strewn about, while the second room was to be used for bone collection and study. I stuck my head into both rooms just to see the layout. Neither room had chairs.

There was a myriad of jobs to be done, even by someone as relatively inexperienced as I was. I did some of the actual digging, something not permitted at the dig in Scole because of the importance of that particular site.

On hands and knees, as I had seen so often at the other digs, I uncovered numerous metal coffin fittings, all that was left of the disintegrated wooden caskets. There were piles of disconnected bones to be found and on one occasion I dug up a skull.....excuse me.....half a skull. It had been sheared right down the middle (when some of the church expansion took place, I was told). I gave a small yelp when I lifted the skull, expecting the heft of the whole skull, and it suddenly sprang free in my hands. A few looked up to see what had happened but most quickly returned to what they were doing. Someone in charge came over and gently carried my spectacular (to me, anyway) find into the bone room, where the tables were gradually filling up with bones laid out as near as possible to their own groupings.

I spent one of my more exciting days at the site with a local doctor who had volunteered his services to the Archaeological Society of Kent. He would be identifying all the bones and I was to be his assistant. I must admit that I got pretty good at the job. Once identified, all the leg bones went

Digging In

into several large, clear-plastic bags while the arm bones were stored in others. We identified finger bones and toe bones. They all went into the same bag. Skulls, even half skulls, went into separate bags.

I had lots of stories to tell Andrea and the boys when I arrived home each evening, and kept them all spellbound with my "skeleton tales from the basement" as I did the chores. There weren't many of the usual non-stop questions from Cameron and Graeme; they just sat and listened and ate.

The time flew by, and before the work in the church was completed I had to be on my way. It was party time!

I drove from Otford to Cardiff on the motorway that had now become as familiar to me as any road I had driven in America. I had driven back and forth over it more times than I wished to count. I had, more or less, also become somewhat accustomed to driving on the 'wrong' side and shifting with my left hand.

The party was held at the Barry Hotel in Barry, Wales about ten miles south of Cardiff, and walking distance to where my camper had been parked the previous year. The guests came from all over England and Wales, and the hotel manager gave the party guests a special rate. It was cheaper staying at the hotel than it would have been staying in the campground, which I would not have done under any circumstances, since I love being close to the action.

I checked in, picked up my room key, and had no trouble finding my relatively unadorned, but comfortable room (that had seen better days) on the main floor. On one side of the double bed I laid out the clothes I planned to wear. Since it was early and the festivities would not start for several hours, I took a long, hot shower and relaxed on the bed for an hour. When I heard people milling around in the halls, I dressed quickly. I

Chasing the Lost Dream

put on a little eye shadow and some lipstick and went out to meet the crowd.

It had been just over a year since I had seen my friends, and since Don had only seen me in my camping gear he didn't recognize me, even after I smiled and said "hello" to him. He said "hello" back, but his eyes showed nothing in the way of recognition. When Marjorie came over and hugged me Don followed to find out who I was. He took a second look and his eyes suddenly glowed. He finally hugged me, kissed my cheek and launched into conversation.

Seeing Marjorie and Don was one of the highlights of the entire trip to England.

Since Barry was a small seacoast village, the birthday party was the talk of the town with a write-up in the local newspaper welcoming special guests and, of course, the birthday girl. This part of Wales had never been known for its elegance but the red carpet was laid out for this event. The champagne flowed and when it flowed into my glass, I made sure that not a drop was wasted!

We danced until the wee hours of the morning. I knew many of the invited guests since we had all wintered in Spain for a couple of years, and several of the men, single or not, seemed to want to dance with 'the foreign lady.' It was close to four in the morning when I returned to my room. I wasn't the last to leave but the others were pretty well oiled and not talking much. I don't think anyone really noticed when I left.

The party resumed the next morning with a champagne breakfast. Although a few of the guests left shortly after breakfast, many of the others stayed. The festivities lasted another three days. I stayed a day or two after all the other guests had left, and Marjorie and Don and I did a lot of talking, some reminiscing and a little crying. After everything was said we kissed goodbye and left, heading in different directions.

Digging In

Marjorie and Don returned to their apartment in Welshpool, Powys in Mid-Wales and I drove back to Bill and Jean Higgs in Temple Cloud, south of Bristol.

Chapter 21

In The End

For the two weeks that I stayed in Temple Cloud I advertised the van in the local newspaper, along with a larger ad with a black-and-white photo in the Buy and Sell Magazine hoping for someone special to come along. I wanted someone who would love the little "puddle jumper" as much as Paul and I had. I waited by the phone.

The Higgs and the Webbs listened to my stories and were in awe of my adventures. I had been in England for a little more than three months. I had traveled all over the country. I had camped in the van for short periods of time. I had worked on three archaeological digs. I had done all the things that I said I was going to do and had survived to tell the story. I could even smile.

"When you first arrived," said Barb "you tried to sound so brave and yet you spoke with a voice that was so shaky we all knew you were terrified. We worried and talked about you every day that you were gone."

"We are so proud of you," said Jean. "You really are brave. Even in my own country I don't know if I could have done what you did."

They were right. I had done it and I was proud of myself. I had returned in three short months a changed person. Much of my confidence had been restored.

Just about the time that I was ready to pack it in for the evening Glynn's friend, whom I hadn't seen since my arrival in the country and couldn't understand at all, and whose name I learned was Lionel, returned for another evening of pleasantries. The conversation bobbed back and forth between

Digging In

Glynn and his visitor, and I was flabbergasted to realize that I understood every word he was saying this time. In that same instant, I realized why I hadn't understood him the first time around. It was not only his accent, one that I had not heard in any other part of the country, but it was the way he spoke that really confused me. Not two sentences in a row were connected to each other. One sentence was about cars; the next sentence was about horses; there was a sentence or two about his job. He talked about what was going on at the local pub and what was going on in his hometown. He sounded like someone was pulling a string at the back of his head and a different subject spewed out each time. Glynn would answer with one or two words before Lionel would be off and running in yet another direction. I would not have been able to follow his conversation even if he spoke American English, which was a far cry from the English that he did speak.

When Lionel left I looked at Jean and laughed: "It's time to go home," I said, without preamble.

In the end I realized that I would need more than two weeks to sell the van. There were a few telephone calls but no one who actually came to see the little home on wheels. I put it back into storage, awaiting another trip. I knew that my traveling days were not over.

In fact, they were just beginning!

Epilogue

Digging In

We all left together, driving slowly east on East Court Road. Jean rode with me, since she seemed to know the back roads to get to the highway and Bill followed in his van. In tandem we drove back to Cardiff and then south to the Barry docks.

I drove into a different part of the yard because I didn't want to be anywhere close to the sap-laden trees that had caused me so much grief. I went into the office where Roger Bennett and I chatted for a few minutes. I spoke briefly about my adventures. He didn't say much, but watched me intently and just smiled sweetly. I gave him the keys, paid for another year of storage, and asked if he wouldn't mind starting it from time to time. I promised I would be back the next year.

Bill and Jean and I then drove back towards Temple Cloud. We stopped for a late lunch in a pub and I had one last Ploughman's Platter with raisin chutney, something that had become a relatively mild and harmless addiction.

We spent my few remaining days reminiscing and talking about what I would do next. I really didn't have a clue as to what I really wanted to do but I promised my friends that I would return. At a local travel agency we picked up a bus ticket for my trip from Bristol to Gatwick. We all cried as I left.

The entire trip, from day one to the last minute, was a gut-wrencher. Perhaps it was a trip that I shouldn't have taken by myself.....or so soon after Paul's death. But I did it. I needed to know for myself that I am one tough broad.....even if it is just on the outside.

Chasing the Lost Dream

Digging In

Turkey in the Middle

Czeching Out

Chapter 1

Preparing for the Outside World

It really was not my intention to go back!

The first trip to this land of enchantment, Turkey, had been marvelous beyond my wildest dreams. It was a place where strangers took you home to meet their family and you felt perfectly safe in going. I loved the exotic balalaika music that accompanied dancers who wore veils and colorful gauzy costumes while performing the seductive belly dance and, of course, in my dreams that dancer was me. It was a land where natives built their homes right into the side of a mountain, and where sarcophagi lay in the middle of the road demanding that you go around them. For me, it had been magic and I knew that it was a trip that could never have been repeated no matter how hard I tried. But I had no choice. I had to go back.

*   *   *   *

I was in my emerald green Ford escort wagon heading for Canada from my condo in Sarasota, Florida at a fairly good clip, driving the seventeen hundred miles in three days. I allowed my mind the luxury of daydreaming about the next six months that I would be spending wandering the villages, towns, cities and countryside of Vietnam, a destination that had conjured up enticing images for several years. All I needed was a few days in Toronto to take care of all the little incidentals that demanded my attention every year. Then I would be heading overseas to new and exotic places.

I had read all the guidebooks that I could find in the library. I exercised my mind by learning to convert Canadian

Chasing the Lost Dream

and U.S. dollars into Vietnamese dong and I must confess that I was getting pretty good at it. I didn't want a repeat of my trip to Turkey where I sat paralyzed at the Dalaman airport trying to figure out what one hundred and eighteen thousand Turkish lira meant in Canadian dollars or one hundred and twenty-seven thousand Turkish lira to the U.S. dollar.

Once I arrived in Toronto I would be staying with my brother Harry and sister-in-law Sandra for about a week or so. I needed to have Phil, a good friend of my late husband's, do my income tax. My teeth needed X-raying and a thorough cleaning and whatever else needed doing. I needed a not-too-close eyeballing from my doctor to make sure that all my parts were in working order and where they should be and, most importantly, I had to renew the mortgage with the woman who had purchased our last home in the Beach area of downtown Toronto. I wanted to visit Sam, my next door neighbor at the wool store I closed in 1989, so I could get one last half-decent haircut. Last, but not least, I would check the prices of a return ticket to Great Britain and buy one of those last-minute flights that bounced you around all night. I couldn't believe that I was doing this again but traveling all night was so much cheaper than traveling at more convenient times. I felt I had months to recuperate from jet lag.

Every trip I had ever taken on my own started, and ended, with visiting my dear friends Bill and Jean Higgs in Temple Cloud, twelve miles south of Bristol. That part of my journey was a must.

They prepared me for the outside world.

Chapter 2

My Light Bulb Moment

On day one of the rest of my life, since it was late in the afternoon having gotten caught in way-too-early-to-be-leaving-work rush hour traffic, I celebrated my Toronto arrival quietly and without fanfare with Harry and Sandra.

The next morning I was up before the sun, anxious to get my chores sorted in order of importance. I monopolized the phone from the instant the caffeine hit that perfect spot that engaged my brain and allowed my mouth to spew out pearls of wisdom. I called everyone I liked (friends) or needed (business associates) in my little black book to let them know that I was back in town temporarily and was ready for lunches and/or dinners out, coffee dates and/or shopping sprees, movies and/or just sitting around talking. Unfortunately, before my social calendar was all organized for my week or ten-day stay, my perfect world crumbled and ground into dust.

The person whose mortgage I held in my hot little hands decided that instead of renewing it, which would have been a simple affair, she would pay me off. She decided that she wanted to deal with a bank close to home rather than with me who would be gallivanting halfway around the world.

Our two or three times a day telephone conversations became utterly tedious. As she didn't know with whom she could share the information she bored me to death with each minute detail of each minute decision. She had called every bank in her area, along with the credit union where she worked and over the next ten day period had appointments with all of them. She wanted the best possible deal, which I could

Chasing the Lost Dream

understand, as interest rates were on the way down, and all the banks were competing for her business.

Blah, blah, blah.....her incessant chatter built up the earwax in both ears until I was totally deaf to her plight. All I wanted was to get out. I had been stuck in Florida all winter long dreaming about traveling the world like an heiress.....or at least like an aging hippie....whatever six dollars a day would get me. Whatever my plans had been, they were put on hold faster than flipping off a light switch. I had to wait until the payoff.

I wanted to spit!

*   *   *   *

After living alone for the past several years, life with Harry and Sandra was a teeth-gnashing experience of trying to keep my temper in check and my mouth shut to the point of smoke coming out of my ears. We three together were explosive; however, I must be fair.

In the summer that my husband Paul had died in the campground in Northern Germany I had gone to live with Harry and Sandra from mid July to early November with only a three-week break to return to Wales to ensure that my camper was secure. During the darkest months of my life and in the deepest depression imaginable they had both been the most kind, generous and caring people on the face of the earth.

The following year when I returned from Florida before going back to England to spend my summer on several archaeological digs Harry and Sandra were very tolerant. In both cases my state of mind was extremely fragile. I knew it and they knew it. They again treated me very kindly. And, in both instances, we all knew that I definitely was not going to be staying long.

Turkey in the Middle

I also had a short visit with them before spending five months in England, Turkey, the Greek Islands and Cyprus, and then again before driving solo to Alaska. They were used to me by now.

This latest development was totally unexpected. I didn't want to be there for an extended period of time anymore than they wanted me there for an extended period of time. We clashed frequently and mostly over the little things that drive everyone over the brink.

I did the crossword puzzle in the newspaper every morning because I was up at five when the paper was delivered. That lasted only a couple of days before Harry told me, through clenched teeth, that the puzzle was the only reason he subscribed to the paper. After a couple of mumbled curses and eyebrow knitting I told him I wouldn't do them anymore.

The coffeepot didn't have an on/off light and when they came home from work one day the apartment reeked of smoke. Yes, it was my fault and yes, I did replace the coffeepot. The new one had an on/off switch with a light that glowed brothel red and was bright enough to light up the entire kitchen, read by or do the crossword puzzle in its glow. Even I could tell when it was on or off.

The parking situation was another thing that drove me to peek over the brink of my sanity and consider jumping. I needed special passes that Harry had to pick up from the apartment manager so they wouldn't tow my car away between ten at night and five in the morning. The daily passes were extremely expensive and not worth the paper they were printed on but, once again, I had no choice.

I got last pick of television programs, not good for a television junkie, and from the instant Harry came home he watched the stock prices rise and fall across the bottom of the

Chasing the Lost Dream

screen. Like I said......it was the little things that drove us all crazy.

Back to the mortgage situation and my reason for feeling like a gerbil without a wheel. When the bank was finally chosen and the mortgage arranged it was time for the accountants and the lawyers to get involved. By the time everything was in order and I had spent half my waking hours in downtown Toronto, struggling with traffic and high prices, two months had gone by. I was not a happy camper.

During my many afternoons alone in the apartment I worked on my second book called *Everyone's Dream Everyone's Nightmare*, about my travels with my late husband, Paul. A realization hit me: on my first trip to Turkey I had put down pages and pages of notes, written a couple of poems, taken roles of pictures, and picked up a handful of brochures. If I expected those notes to become a book I had better do it sooner rather than later. Too much time had already elapsed. I suddenly realized that I had to go back to Turkey - where better to write about Turkey than in Turkey?

That was my light bulb moment. I have no idea what I was smoking or sniffing when I came up with that bright idea!

Chapter 3

Money, Money, Money.....Do the Problems Ever End

A few days before my departure for 'across the puddle' as my husband used to call it, I called the Higgs/Webb household in the hopes that I could inform Jean of my plans, who in turn, would be excited enough to tell everyone else in the household or within earshot range about my impending arrival. Barb Webb was the only person home.

I told her that I would be arriving sometime during the next week. That was really all the information she needed or wanted, and since I didn't have my ticket yet it was all I could tell her. I needed to be sure that all the bits and pieces had been taken care of, and would not dissolve under closer scrutiny, before I purchased one of those last minute flights.

That same day I called my investment broker and asked for a check in the amount of four thousand dollars. I would use it to purchase traveler's checks. I picked up the check early the next morning from the downtown office and, within minutes was on the subway heading back up north.

I took the check to the Royal Bank branch closest to my brother's apartment. They wouldn't cash it because it wasn't 'my branch' even though I had enough money in the account to cover that check with money left over to buy a house, a car, a pony, lunch in a fancy restaurant or to pay for parking in downtown Toronto.

I took the check to the Canadian Automobile Club and tried to purchase four thousand dollars worth of traveler's checks with it: they wouldn't accept it. They would allow only three thousand dollars worth of checks to be purchased with my personalized check. This whole money, money, money affair

Chasing the Lost Dream

was starting to really annoy me. Deep down my gut was a volcano ready to erupt.

I purchased three thousand dollars worth of traveler's checks with my personal check then returned to the Royal Bank and deposited the four thousand dollar check into my account. I would definitely be short of money once I got overseas but I was anxious to get out of town and frustrated with all the little details and delays that I never experienced on any of my other trips.

I continued with more of the last minute preparations. I picked up the two pairs of glasses that I ordered 'just in case' and went home, frustrated but eager for the next step in this problem-filled trip.

The next morning was (finally) ticket-buying time. I called one of the "last minute clubs" among the many that were listed in the newspaper and asked if they had a flight to London, I didn't care which airport. I was promptly advised that I had to give them my Visa or Mastercard number before they could check. In short I had to 'join' the last minute club before they would check on flights.

"What happens," I asked "if you don't have a ticket available?"

"Well," he replied " then we will issue a credit."

"I really don't feel comfortable giving you my Visa number without some assurance that you have an available ticket for me," I said.

"Lady," he said rather crudely, "blow it out your ear."

Needless to say I wasn't too impressed with the friendly service from that particular company and decided that it wasn't worth my time calling back to speak with a manager. I'm sure Mr. Blow-in-my-Ear-and-I'll-Follow-you-Anywhere was not planning on "travel agent" as a career, and would be gone before my complaint ever reached a person in authority.

Turkey in the Middle

I purchased my ticket later that afternoon with a travel agency that specialized in flights to Britain. Since this was the latest I had ever left Canada to go overseas, end of June, I paid a whopping six hundred and twenty-six dollars for the ticket, at least two hundred more than usual.

With a valid ticket tucked away in my pocket I was almost ready for lift-off. I started counting the minutes. The next day I was down to the wire with last minute chores. I did my laundry, wrote a few letters, made a bunch of phone calls and cleaned up my little part of the world.

Monday the twenty-fourth of June was one of those long, endless days filled with insignificant stuff. I was just trying to keep busy doing nothing. I was packed and ready to go. I went for a couple of long walks with my friend Pearl; I mailed the letters I had written the day before. I went out to lunch with my friend Eva. At the supermarket I purchased munchies, mostly hard candies that I stuffed into my carry-on luggage and would eat all the way to London.

This was the first time in all my travels that there was no one to take me to the airport, to send me off in a grand style or to just wave as they left me at the departure door. Despite my wanting to head out on another adventure my heart was heavy.

When it was time I slowly made my way to the York Mills Subway Station where I purchased a ticket to the airport for the sum of eight dollars and fifty cents. There were three of us on the bus. When we stopped at Yorkdale, a huge shopping complex in the heart of uptown Toronto, to pick up other passengers, the bus suddenly ballooned with people and luggage and backpacks.

Kathy Evans, a neatly dressed woman in her forties, sat beside me, and in chatting I discovered that we were both going to London's Gatwick Airport. We were actually to be on the same flight.

Chasing the Lost Dream

We arrived at the airport, checked our bags through to London and learned that our flight would be leaving at one-fifteen the next morning instead of eleven forty-five that night. Disappointed, Kathy and I roamed the airport looking at everything there was to look at and purchasing nothing. We talked until we were hoarse. We read the back cover of every book on the shelf in the kiosk store and finally went back to check on the flight. In the end we sat side-by-side staring straight ahead and moaning to each other until the plane was ready to receive us.

The flight was smooth and uneventful but I couldn't sleep which definitely added to my unpleasant mood. When breakfast finally arrived, (I felt as if I had waited up all night for it) it was inedible. I couldn't eat the quiche and sausage, if that is indeed what it was. Had the stewardess told me that it was cardboard or packing material that we were eating I would have had no reason to doubt her. I wrapped the bun and muffin in my napkin and put them in my purse for later. I hoped that when the nausea, due to fatigue, had subsided I would eat anything that was handy.

I said goodbye to Kathy at customs, wished her a great trip and we went our separate ways in the airport lobby. The room was crowded but I knew that no one was there waiting for me. Still I couldn't help but look out at the sea of people hoping for a familiar face.

Right outside the front door I discovered that the bus to Bristol would be leaving within five minutes. I felt like I was in the American Express commercial sprinting through the airport like O.J. Simpson. I paid for my bus ticket with American money because there was no time to get Sterling. I had no cash to buy anything on the bus. I ate the bun and muffin, now hard as a rock and tasteless without butter or jelly, along with the few candies that I had left in my bag. I was fully awake during the

Turkey in the Middle

entire trip and was in a slightly better mood when I arrived in Bristol.

I left my bags behind the desk at the Bristol bus terminal. I found a Barclay's bank, withdrew two hundred pounds in British Sterling, and felt solvent. I retrieved my bags, hopped on the bus to Temple Cloud, paid my one-pound ten, and took the first seat I could find.

A war-weary type of fatigue descended upon me!

Chapter 4

When Will I Ever Learn

She introduced herself as Milly. She was in her mid-twenties with dull, straight blond hair, sallow complexion and what I think of as a typically English tooth problem. Her two front teeth protruded even when her mouth was closed which wasn't often on this trip.

Milly was chipper and her enthusiasm kept me awake and talking. There wasn't a quiet moment until I got off the bus in front of the post office in Temple Cloud. Without her I'm sure I would have succumbed to a brain-dead daze for the entire trip, short though it was, and would probably have snoozed through my stop. I waved as I stood on the sidewalk. She smiled back, the tips of her fingers wiggling at me from an inch above the window ledge.

At the first lull in the fast moving traffic I ran across the street, luggage bumping and bouncing along behind me hitting every pebble and stray twig under its tiny wheels. It was a short walk down the main street of Temple Cloud to the almost invisible turnoff, but I had taken that particular bend in the road on several other visits so I found it easily enough. It was one of the shortest streets I had ever been on, not more than twenty paces, and I'm not even sure it had a name but thankfully I knew it by sight. There was also a slight incline and I was well beyond exhaustion so any molehill became a mountain. The walk to Cloud Hill Farm was tortuous.

Although I had only one large, overstuffed bag, thankfully on wheels, and an easy-to-handle knapsack so light that I could hardly feel it strapped to my back, it was still almost too much to bear. I trudged slowly down East Court Road until

Turkey in the Middle

home....or what would be my home for as long as I chose to stay.

I opened the side gate. The white rabbit was still in its hutch and although I glanced its way I didn't get too close, knowing that it was prone to biting the hand that fed it! The garden, running against the side wall from the house to the bottom fence, was in full bloom with rows of carrots, capsicum, lettuce and cabbage. There were mounds of zucchini, several large enough to be used as baseball bats and I picked one to let my friends know that I was ready to help clean out the garden. There were so many lengthy strings of runner beans, Bill's favorite, that I couldn't count them all, particularly with eyes at half-mast that crossed and uncrossed with each blink.

I knocked on the back door and stepped into the enclosed summer deck where we usually ate our meals when there were just a few of us or when it was too warm to sit in the kitchen. I left my luggage in the hallway near the stairs so I could grab them on the way up. I knocked on the kitchen door, opened it and peeked inside. The first to hug me was Bill, Jean's husband, followed by Barb and Glynn, registered owners of the two-storey brick house.

They were just sitting down to dinner and, with just a few quick moves, room was made for me in the middle of the group. I was grateful that I wouldn't have to shout from one end of the huge dinner table to the other. Whatever the conversation was it stopped immediately upon my arrival. I told them about my trip. I really didn't have to tell them how tired I was. They could see it in my eyes that had become soft and droopy and heard it in my voice. I had started strong but halfway through dinner I could barely get the words out. My shoulders slumped and I fought to stay awake.

I couldn't even pretend to help clean up. Bill washed, dried and put the dishes in the cupboard and Barb insisted that I

Chasing the Lost Dream

head upstairs. I didn't need much convincing. I took my luggage up to the third floor where my bedroom was, right next to Bill and Jean's. I dropped it on the floor, changed into comfy clothes and headed down to the second floor to take a long, leisurely bath. By the time Bill came up the stairs I was sound asleep on the couch. He didn't disturb me, but left the television set on and went to bed sometime before I got up. I awoke about twelve-thirty in the morning, turned off the television set and headed for bed. It took me a while to fall back asleep but when I finally did I don't think I moved the rest of the night. I awoke at the crack of noon.

I knew instantly what day it was. My husband Paul had died exactly four years before in a campground in Northern Germany. I didn't want to dwell on the date.

Bill and I had coffee and then breakfast or lunch, depending on who was eating. We talked little, especially when I reminded him of the date. I waited for Jean. Bill was even more anxious than I was to see her.

She arrived early afternoon from a ten-day holiday in Wales with their daughter Debra. We spent the next few days playing catch up, talking about old and new times. We took long walks. We played scrabble most nights and just plain, old relaxed, allowing me time to get used to the time change. In addition to helping with daily chores I took care of my own needs.

I made an appointment with Jean's doctor for a hepatitis shot on the following Monday. From the doctor's office, where I was made a temporary resident so I wouldn't have to pay for the shot, Jean and I drove into downtown Bristol, a drive that was slow and dusty due to road repair. I purchased my plane ticket to Dalaman from Cardiff, Wales. It was by far the cheapest but I wouldn't have done it if Jean hadn't insisted that they would drive me to Cardiff.

Turkey in the Middle

The drive home was even more hellish than the drive to Bristol. It took close to two hours to drive the twelve miles. I worried all the way about seeing Bill's face when Jean told him that they were driving me to Cardiff. I was stunned to discover that he was thrilled. They both loved having places to go to, and the better the reason for going, the more they enjoyed the trip.

On departure day Jean and I did a little grocery shopping, and I did my last load of laundry in a real machine and hung it out on a real line to dry. I took one last nap in front of the television set. We played scrabble one last time and since I won every game I'm sure they were anxious for me to get on the road. Late in the afternoon we took the one-and-a-half hour drive to Cardiff. They graciously waited the three hours with me until it was time to board the plane.

I know I've said this before and I know I'll be saying it again sometime in the not-too-distant future but I'm really getting too old for these all-night flights.....

Chapter 5

My Unheralded Arrival

Unlike the gut-wrenching terror that had afflicted me on my first trip to Turkey when I had boldly gone where no one in my family circle had gone before or ever wanted to go before, there was none of that on this trip. This trip was blissfully uneventful for me so far. The plane was full which meant I had to sit up straight all night, unlike the first flight that had been empty due to bombs going off in two of the major cities that I was to visit. On that trip I released two armrests and stretched out on three seats waking up ten minutes later when panic set in and I started to hyperventilate. On this flight I was forced to be a perfect Miss Manners and I know my parents would have been proud of my posture.

Any tension and frustration I felt was due to the number of children on board, all of ankle-biting age. They had been so unbearably loud, and, as we have all experienced at one time or another in our lives, in the middle of the night a pin dropping on a shag carpet is loud. The whole lot of them had been whiny and cranky and frankly I was whiny and cranky myself with no mama or papa around on whom to vent my frustration. Within minutes of take-off I looked forward to snapping my fingers like an aged genie and landing in Turkey, strapping on the gear and parachuting into neutral territory or just plain opening the door and throwing myself to the wolves.

It was a smooth, middle of the night (five o'clock) landing. Unlike the last trip, when I held my passport up over my head and was ushered through customs quickly and efficiently with only one or two dignitaries in front of me to slow me down, this time I felt like I had just left a cattle car and

Turkey in the Middle

my branding didn't warrant anything close to special treatment. I now had to wait in an unending line to obtain a visa and the visa had to be paid for with money from the country of origin. Thankfully I had a twenty-dollar American bill in my belly pouch that I had no idea I would be needing at the airport.

Once I was through customs and out into the lobby I met John and Maggie, a thirty-ish couple from Britain, and Meghan, a twenty-something young woman from New Zealand who was teaching English in Japan and vacationing in Turkey. It didn't take us long to get acquainted, decide which way we were all headed and make a decision. We reviewed our options and decided, since we were all going in the same general direction, which was south, to share a taxi to Fethiye. We piled into an awaiting taxi after jamming all the various sizes and shapes of our luggage into the trunk and negotiating the price with the driver. I held my knapsack on my lap, since things were a little crammed in the back, and patted my belly pouch just to make sure it was securely fastened under my shirt.

I watched the familiar scenery zip by, not saying much. As a matter of fact, no one said much. It had been a long flight for everyone and we just wanted to get where we were going and hopefully into the embrace of a comfy bed for a late morning or early afternoon nap.

I was let out first, right in front of my favorite local "pansyion" (family owned and operated bed and breakfast), called, of all things, The Sinderella Pansyion. I stood there stunned and staring for just a moment, realizing how much easier this trip was compared to my first.

Despite the excitement and novelty of it all, my first trip had been a constant struggle. I only spoke one language fluently: English, with just a smattering of French and even less German. The money made absolutely no sense to me. I had no idea where I would stay or how I would negotiate for the rooms

Chasing the Lost Dream

once I got one. I had a genuine distrust of the people. There were so many other problems that went along with being alone in a strange country for the first time.....and being scared.

This trip was so different. I was now a seasoned traveler, used to being on my own. At least at the start, this second trip was a breeze.

The drive had taken a couple of hours, and I was the only one let out at that particular stop. The rest had gone on to the Tourist Information Center in town to find accommodations.

It was still early morning but Ahmet, the owner, was asleep on a table in the courtyard, his leg encased in a pure white plaster cast, crutches by his side. I hesitated for another brief moment then swung open the gate and walked over to him. He opened his eyes like he was just resting them rather than awakening from a dead-sleep. There was an almost instant recognition and he wasn't shy about giving me a hug and a kiss on the cheek.

He called for coffee, which was brought out before I sat down, and told me a room would be ready in about an hour or so. Several of the guests would be leaving and a room on the main floor would be cleaned. I asked for Sema.

It had been two years since my last trip. Sema, a dark-haired beauty and former airline hostess for Turkish Airways, and the mother of their four-year-old son, had divorced Ahmet the year before and was living in Antalya. I would miss her. She had made my Fethiye experience a delightful adventure. I don't think Ahmet missed her. He was too busy telling me about all of his conquests over the past year.

"Did one of your lady-friends or perhaps one of their husbands break your leg?" I asked.

"No," he replied solemnly, not seeing or enjoying my sense of humor, "it was a motorcycle accident."

Turkey in the Middle

I was not surprised at the divorce. I knew she was unhappy when I was there even though she didn't talk much about it. Ahmet had always had an "eye" for the ladies and I suspected that he acted upon that "eye" more than once. I was just sorry that I wouldn't be seeing her. She had made Ahmet tolerable and, although not always terribly pleasant, he had always made female guests, especially those traveling alone, feel protected in his pansyion.

Just about the time that Ahmet had kind of made my skin crawl with his rude and crude language and the description of the numbers of women that were vying for his attention, my room was ready. I left immediately and was grateful for the break.

I set my luggage down on one bed, spreading out a few things and hanging up a few more items that were already wrinkled. I finally laid my travel-weary body down on the second bed, releasing an audible sigh of relief. It was still relatively cool and deathly quiet. It didn't take long to fall asleep. I slept peacefully for about three hours.

I hate all night flights.....but I think I mentioned that before.

Chapter 6

Looking For Friends

Before the day was out I was wandering around in downtown Fethiye hoping to see a familiar face or two. There weren't any amongst the tourist population. There were a few shopkeepers that I recognized but they didn't remember me; so I continued wandering, looking in store windows, and hoping to strike up conversations with the locals or tourists.

They were just uncovering some new ruins in the harbor and although they weren't working this particular day it was worth walking the perimeter of the site. There were mounds of dirt, with imbedded rocks, thick twisted metal rods and concrete pieces everywhere. Tripping or slipping would be easy so I tried to be careful. From the closest shopkeeper I learned that they would be continuing the dig when they could get more money. I knew that it wouldn't be anytime while I was still in the area. Money was so hard to come by.

By late afternoon I was back at the pansyion hoping that some interesting people had arrived while I was away. Cleo was in her late twenties, single, rail-thin and from a part of Britain where the language could not be easily understood except by someone from her own region. A Dutch couple in their mid-twenties had also arrived as well as Mehmet, a boy in his late teens from a small village in the interior of Turkey who, for the first time, wanted to see what the ocean looked like. There was interesting dinner conversation. None of the other guests had been to this part of Turkey before so I was able to act as a tour guide, giving information about where to go, what to see and approximately what it would cost to get there.

Turkey in the Middle

Of course everything would be much cheaper for Mehmet, as I discovered on my last trip, because tourists paid high Turkish lira prices for all entrance fees while locals paid a fraction of the cost. Considering the poverty in this country I felt that was fair.

Even at that early 'brain-addled-by-fatigue' date I remembered that my main purpose in coming to Turkey was to write the book about my adventures there two years earlier. But I would still be keeping notes on this current trip. I had discussed the book with Ahmet and had made some notes. Small sections had already been put to paper in short story form. Ahmet loved the tales I wrote about and was thrilled when I mentioned coming back to Fethiye to visit friends. Every time someone new would come into the courtyard Ahmet would insist that I read that section over and over again. He also insisted on them knowing that HE was the friend I was writing about. He was completely oblivious to the fact that it was his (former) wife I was really writing about.....but why stir the pot?

Without Sema to talk to, the grounded, levelheaded, even-tempered, caring one of the partnership, I didn't want to stay long. I must admit, however, that I was impressed with the fact that Ahmet, with one quick telephone call, had arranged for the Kaş bus to pick me up at the front door of the pansyion. What I was not impressed with were the kisses he expected as a thank you.

"Don't they shoot horses with broken legs?" I asked him. He responded with a blank look and a skimpy smile.

I was on the bus heading south when I met Jean-Luc, a young French-Canadian from Laval, Quebec. He had been traveling through Turkey for the past four months and would be staying at Smiley's. It seems that in my two-year absence Smiley had opened the second floor of his restaurant to

Chasing the Lost Dream

backpackers. It was a free room as long as you ate your meals in his establishment. I learned that during the winter months his hostel was full to overflowing, as was his restaurant.

With a pleasant companion, from my home province no less, and chitchat all the way, the familiar scenery and being alert enough to enjoy it, the trip was over before I realized it. We wished each other good luck and parted at the bus depot.

After running into Jean-Luc on the main street in Kaş later that day I learned that Smiley's hostel was full and my young friend needed a reasonable room someplace. I told him that it would not be difficult; Kaş was filled with rooms of every shape, size, description and most importantly, price range. "Just keep bargaining," I told him. "They'll come down in price."

Arranging my own place to stay had been super simple. I left the bus depot at the top of the main street and was walking carefully down the broken and pot-holed sidewalk towards town. Everything looked so familiar and inviting that I had to smile. I felt like I was home and I loved the feeling. With my luggage in tow, I went looking for my friends Michael Henderson and Stephen Butler, who lived on the second storey in a small apartment right on the main street. I was just a block or so away from where I was headed when I heard "madam.....madam.....madam" being called.

I turned to see a familiar face beaming at me, Urso. Two years before he had arranged a room for me at the Oba Pansyion and was now asking if I needed a room. "Yes," I replied and before he could say another word I untied my one piece of luggage from the wheeled carrier, opened my luggage, and stowed the carrier inside and tossed him my bag. I kept the knapsack on my back. I told him what I was willing to pay and he didn't seem to want to argue.

116

Turkey in the Middle

"I'll see you in a couple of hours" I said, and was off before he could say another word. I was so excited about the prospect of seeing Stephen and Michael again.

I found their apartment and knocked on the door. A middle-aged woman with a small child wrapped around her leg opened it just wide enough for me to see half her body. She spoke only a little English; my friends had moved, and she didn't know where I could find them.

Chapter 7

Turkish Life

I walked back to the street where the Oba Pansyion stood and was delighted to see my friend Urso, the same Urso whom I had given my luggage to, waving to me from the Gunus Pansyion. It seems in my haste and excitement I had forgotten to ask which pansyion he worked for. I had simply assumed that he was still at Oba. Fortunately he had the good sense to wait and watch for me. I might still be wandering around Turkey today looking for my luggage had he not been so diligent.

The room he had available for me was clean with fresh linen on the bed, and smelled newly painted; but it was smaller than any room I had ever seen in Turkey or anyplace else for that matter. I've owned houses with closets that were larger than this room. It had two windows, one on the side where the headboard was and the other overlooking the balcony. The balcony was short, extremely narrow and would accommodate only one chair. I would either have to sit sideways or prop my feet up on the railing. Either way suited me. With two windows I was assured of feeling even the gentlest of breezes.

The room was on the second floor so I wouldn't mind leaving the windows open when I wasn't there. I really didn't know how long I would be staying and if I chose to stay for a couple of months I would re-negotiate the price since it was not worth what I was paying.....about six dollars a night.

I opened my soft-sided bag and removed a few things that I didn't want too wrinkled. I hung them up on the bathroom doorknobs, both inside and out, since there wasn't any other place to hang stuff. The rest of my clothing I left in the bag and had to climb over it every time I wanted to go from

Turkey in the Middle

the bathroom to the balcony. There were no drawers either except for the tiny top drawer of a side table. I put my toiletries on the sink ledge in the bathroom.

I took a quick shower, dried, dressed in a matter of minutes and, once again, went looking for my friends. "Someone will know where Stephen and Michael moved to," I mumbled under my breath, "assuming of course, that they still lived someplace in or around Kaş. Oh, yuk," I said out loud as I left my room, "what happens if they went back to England?"

I said "hello" to Apo, my favorite waiter at Café Corner, where I ate breakfast and lunch every day while in Kaş. He greeted me with a peck on the cheek. That's not to say he recognized me, he was just that kind of guy. A little kiss on the cheek for a vaguely familiar, gray-haired woman almost guaranteed him a good tip. He hadn't seen Stephen or Michael that day but assured me that they were still around. I continued my roaming.

I walked up the main drag with its tourist shops on both sides and stone sarcophagi at the top of the street and turned off onto a side street before ever reaching the top. I went into Smiley's Restaurant and the owner recognized me immediately and came over to greet me. He offered a cup of tea, which I appreciated and sipped slowly. Ebo, sitting at another table, looked at me rather blankly. He was in partnership with my friends in the condo building business and eventually figured out who I was. He nodded. I nodded back.

On the way back to Café Corner I ran into Stephen whose eyes widened almost to the point of popping out of his head. He held me out at arms-length to have a good look and to make sure it was really 'me' before squeezing me into a welcoming bear hug. He took no time in finding a phone to call Michael. Michael arrived in less than twenty minutes.

Chasing the Lost Dream

We had dinner at Smiley's, coffee at Café Corner and danced at Red Point until the bottoms of my feet were raw, my ankles were wobbly, and my calves and thighs were sore to the touch. My knees kept giving out, reminding me of my nineteen seventy-four skiing accident; I was quite sure I wouldn't be able to walk home. I kissed them both goodbye and headed out. They stayed for a few more drinks.

As I made my way down the main street and then the side street, I worried that the lights would be out, which frequently happened in many of the older buildings in most of the small towns. Thankfully the place was lit up like a Christmas tree. I trudged up to the second floor and found my door. I turned the light on in my room and a roach, big enough to wear a saddle, scurried under the door to my balcony. It was around two-thirty in the morning at this point, having been a slow, painful walk home.

Since I was still spending my winters in deep-south U.S.A. roaches were nothing out of the ordinary, except of course, they are called palmetto bugs in Florida. Ah yes, a rose by any other name.....a roach is a roach is a cockroach.

It had been a long and very active day. I had imbibed in a couple of glasses of beer and had danced so much that winding down took some time. When the sun was just beginning to show her face, I was finally relaxed enough to fall asleep. I slept like the dead and the sun was high in the sky when I eventually dragged myself out of bed.

I showered, dressed and was having my favorite breakfast of honey, yogurt and diced fruit by eleven in the morning. I asked for a second cup of appletea and didn't feel like moving until I finished. My legs didn't want to cooperate with whatever I had in mind for the day so I just sat there, sipping. Eventually I had to unglue myself from the seat bottom and headed out.

Turkey in the Middle

It didn't take me long to get back into the swing of small town Turkish living. I headed back to my room after my long, relaxing breakfast because there was no one to talk to and very few tourists were out and about during the heat of the day. Locals didn't come out until after sundown.

By late afternoon, with the usual daily chores over with, I was ready to get back out into the tourist world. In my down time I had washed out my clothes from the previous day and secured them onto the balcony railing to dry. I had written a few letters so my friends and family wouldn't worry about me. I had read a couple chapters of whatever novel I was reading. I had organized a few notes for the book I planned on writing and was bored with all of it. I left the building.

Out on the street I ran into Stephen who introduced me to Shirley and Liam from Manchester, now living in Turkey. Kaş had turned, or perhaps it always was and I just hadn't noticed, into the proverbial Peyton Place.

Smiley was almost everyone's favorite topic of gossip. It seems there was a different girlfriend in his life every week or two, usually a foreign tourist since they were in and out of Kaş like the tongue of a frog zapping a fly in midair.

By my second visit to his establishment, and since I now knew what to look for, even I could spot his newest conquest as he saved a favorite table for her in the outdoor section of his restaurant. In between serving customers he would sit with her, sipping a glass of wine or tea or beer or whatever she was drinking. He was not particular.....about anything, obviously.

Occasionally Smiley's wife would be sitting at another table watching the goings-on but she never said anything. Much of her face was covered with a scarf that she held bunched up in her hand so the bruising wouldn't show.

I was getting involved in a different side of Turkish life on this trip.

Chapter 8

Market Day

I was up and out early the next morning because it was market day. Every town had a market on a different day and today was Kaş' turn. Whether I was looking for something in particular or not I loved wandering the three or four congested blocks and going up and down every isle just to see what they had. There were varieties of melon that I had never seen or tasted and every vendor offered healthy-sized samples. Most days I would go home with one or two small ones that I would massacre on my balcony, cutting them open with a tiny penknife that I kept in my bag and scooping out the contents with the same knife. There were vegetables that intrigued me because of their color or size or shape. It was in Turkey that I discovered tiny purple eggplants and spotted beans and Turkish Delight candy that came in a hundred different flavors rather than the red jelly covered in a thin layer of chocolate that I knew so well.

On this particular visit to the market I was hoping to find a mosquito repellent that didn't actually poison me, leaving the mosquitoes alive to suck the remaining life from my body. On the walk home the previous night I had gotten caught on the street with 'fogging' machinery that blanketed the entire town with what was supposed to be a 'death trap' for mosquitoes. The dense fog chased all the live mozzies, as the English like to call those little blood-sucking creatures, into my room. Sadly, after walking up and down the entire length and breadth of the market a couple of times on my quest, I had found nothing in the way of a bug repellent, poisonous or otherwise.

Turkey in the Middle

Although I had been in bed relatively early the previous night, according to Turkish nightlife, I realized that sleep was not going to come easy. From the minute I crawled into bed, around midnight, my hands and arms were in constant motion trying to slap at the mosquitoes that laughed and poked fun at me relentlessly through the night. I'm sure they were high on whatever they had been sprayed with from the fogging equipment and were just out to have a good time, at my expense. Being up and out early with definite plans to take care of the problem prevented me from jumping on the first plane out of there.

Michael was supposed to meet me at our favorite breakfast and drinking hole, Café Corner, with his computer in tow, so I could write my book in the comfort of my own room. He didn't show up. Stephen did. Over a gallon of tea, I sat and listened to the whole story again.

They had had a terrible fight and Michael had taken to his bed. Stephen was close to tears. They had come to Turkey four years before with such high hopes. Both had resigned from good government jobs in England. They brought with them sufficient money to build four condominiums. They would live in one. They would keep one as a rental that would bring in a monthly salary that they could live on and the other two would be sold. They could live like kings for the rest of their lives. That had been the plan and there isn't a person on the planet that is not familiar with "the best laid plans......"

Before they could actually start the business they had to take on a Turkish partner. When I first heard about their plans two years earlier I had cautioned them about taking on a Turkish partner since neither of them spoke Turkish well enough to read legal documents. My words fell on deaf ears.

They had started the construction. They were living in the only finished villa. They had almost no money left. Their

Chasing the Lost Dream

Turkish partner had taken and squandered most of it. Whatever else happened on a daily basis just added to the stress of their home life. Things were not good for my friends.

Stephen and I sat together right through lunch that day. He talked and I listened. Whatever I wanted to say I had said two years earlier. He didn't want advice; he just wanted someone to listen.....so I stayed.

*   *   *   *

Since my arrival I had heard and seen nothing but depressing stories. This was such a very different trip from the first time. It was not pleasant and only added to my stress. I had so looked forward to coming back to Turkey. Now I didn't know if I wanted to stay. In my infinite wisdom, I decided that as long as I continued to write on a daily basis that it would be worthwhile staying since it was my major reason for being there. I must confess that seeing my friends was way up there in my list of reasons for being back in Turkey.

It was while sitting on a bench at the water's edge looking out at the Turquoise Coast that I wrote my first poem, something that I had never attempted before nor even contemplated doing. Within a week I wrote my second poem at a restaurant during dinner one evening. The restaurant, perched on the top of a hill, overlooked the entire city, with stars so low I wanted to reach out and touch them. There was one star in particular that reminded me of Bible stories and I watched until it disappeared.

I met several new people, among them Christine and Dirk who were from Belgium. They were both musicians. They were pleasant and easy-going with a good sense of humor and they made conversation light and interesting. They stayed only one week and didn't stray too far from the town center because

Turkey in the Middle

of a 'titchy tummy' they both picked up from lunch at one of the stalls on Kaputaş Beach.

Ercan and Ebo were twenty-something Turkish businessmen, very westernized and easy to talk to about love, life and the pursuit of happiness. I read them my poems because they asked to hear them. I reviewed some of my book chapters with them and, since my view of their country was so positive, they seemed to enjoy hearing about my rendition of their world.

Paul and Dorothy were my English friends and I could always cry on their shoulders. I met a couple from South Africa who were really enjoying their whirlwind holiday and I wandered up and down several of the side streets with them showing off some of the tombs, the archaeological sites and sarcophagi that were hidden from the main streets. That evening we ended up at an outdoor bar, right off the main street, watching the strangest, ugliest and hairiest-looking belly dancer. Upon closer inspection the belly dancer turned out to be one of the young waiters who had decided to put on a show. Later that night he passed himself off as Diana Ross. Finally.....we had some great belly laughs.

I met a young American woman from South Carolina. She was in her last days of a month long trip. I envied her going home. I told her that I had lots of work to do but would meditate about either staying in Turkey or going someplace else. "I'll leave it up to the universe and see what happens," I told her. At the end of the evening, she wished me good luck and I never saw her again. I promised to write.

There were some friends from the previous trip that I met up with again. Of course, Stephen and Michael were around all the time. I ran into Suzanne Swann from Canada, who was now a journalist and had been living in Turkey for many years.

Chasing the Lost Dream

I ran into Christine Williams, my favorite English tour guide, a time or two wandering around Kaş, and we always stopped to hug and chat. She divided her time between the Black Sea area and Kaş, taking tourists from one to the other and back again and usually on bike tours. She was definitely a favorite amongst the active and physically fit and always had entertaining stories to tell.

Just about the time that I was sick to death of listening to everyone else's problems, I closed my eyes, said a short prayer, asking whether I should stay in Kaş or go elsewhere. I opened my eyes.....expecting nothing.

I could not believe what I was seeing. Coming around the corner looking as neat as a pin in white shorts, baby blue collared tee shirt and carrying his tennis racquet was Chris Berry. He stopped dead in his tracks when he saw me. He gave me a big toothy grin. He walked over, gave me a big hug and sat down.

My prayer was answered!

Chapter 9

Raven

He promised to bring Margaret and Karina to Café Corner that afternoon for drinks and would not tell them that I was back. After some all-too-brief chatting and joking, laughing and catching up on family news with him, he was off for his tennis match with a local doctor, a game he played several times a week.

Chris, Margaret and their daughter Karina had been my port in the storm two years earlier. Among other things they had stowed one bag of luggage under a spare bed when I decided that I didn't need the "ski clothes" that I had brought with me. My Temple Cloud friends, Bill and Jean Higgs along with Barb and Glynn Webb, had told me that it got "cool" in the evening on the Turkish coast. I discovered that "cool" meant the temperature dipped below one hundred degrees…..but not by much.

Chris and Margaret had been there to introduce me to others in the area who spoke English so I wouldn't feel quite so alone. Almost every day, when in town, we had met for afternoon drinks and nibbles at our favorite drinking hole and others gravitated to our table as if being pulled by a giant magnet. They would let me know about events or parties taking place where I would feel comfortable enough to attend on my own. Once at a party, I would always run into others I knew, and before long, I would fit right in.

Several afternoons that year, after freshly brewed coffee and cookies and relaxing on their balcony until we got bored, we would watch old familiar television reruns or they would translate some of the news for me. There was nothing like

Chasing the Lost Dream

watching *Raiders of the Lost Ark* in Turkish. We had great fun when we watched a movie we all knew and while the actors spoke Turkish we translated into English and did more giggling than translating.

Over the course of a couple of years and while on holidays, Karina had met, fallen in love with, and had married a very handsome Turkish fellow, Zuhtu. They now had a four-year-old son by the name of Emin, and although they all lived and worked in Wales they returned to Kaş regularly to visit grandparents. Yes, I had to admit to myself that yet again this family was the answer to my prayers.

So here I was, two years later, waiting impatiently for the group to round the corner. At first glance, except for Chris, they didn't notice me sitting at one of the center tables trying to look nonchalant. It was when Margaret literally bumped my chair that she looked down to say "excuse me" and her eyes lit up first in astonishment and then with excitement.

We chattered on like magpies, each of us taking turns in telling the other what the last two years had been like. The family was fascinated by the turn of events in my life. They loved the fact that I was writing, and although I had had several travel pieces published I was just starting to put my short essays together for a book.

Margaret filled me in on the events of the most recent flight from Cardiff (Wales) to Dalaman (Turkey). Upon boarding, Emin, whose dark flashing eyes and serious demeanor had made him a favorite of all who worked on board, had been given a tiny, plastic toy airplane. Rather than just wheeling it around on the open tray, he had been swooping it into the air and smashing it down on the table, shouting "CRASH" with each nose-dive. He continued to play this way while the faces of the other passengers got paler and paler. The steward finally came over and asked Margaret if she could take the toy away

Turkey in the Middle

from him until he got home. He was "upsetting" the other passengers.

From late afternoon into early evening, visiting with my friends at Café Corner was, literally and figuratively, absolutely delicious from start to finish. A dark-haired beauty joined us a few seconds after realizing that we were speaking English. Her name was Raven, no last name attached to that, and she was from Taos, New Mexico. Except to break for a quick introduction all around the table the lively conversation continued with Raven putting in her two-cents worth when we discussed the buying and selling of Turkish wares.

When Chris, Margaret and Karina went home for dinner Raven and I sat at our same table for a few more drinks and a light meal. Men of every size, shape, color and nationality floated over to our table. Some stayed and joined in the conversation. Some just came over to introduce themselves and stare at Raven.

My new friend was well-traveled, and wanted to do some carpet buying in Turkey and selling to her rich friends in New Mexico, so there was much to hold our attention. Just as Raven and I were getting up to go and try a different coffee place she had heard about, strolling down the main street came Cleo from Fethiye with her friends, Annette and Hilary, whom I had never met.

While we got caught up on where everyone had been for the last few weeks an unexpected blast of cool air wafted over us. It was actually cool enough to require the sweatshirt that I had left in my room and that I had no intention of getting.

The evening ended late.....even later than normal. It must have been around four in the morning when I finally got back to my room. I was used to wending my way back to the pansyion around two along with the rest of the group, but we

129

Chasing the Lost Dream

had all gotten caught up in the liveliest of conversations and no one really wanted to leave.

The next morning Raven and I met for a late breakfast and by early afternoon we met up with a larger group that included Chris and Margaret. We shoehorned ourselves into a couple of taxies and went out to Villa SEM (Stephen, Ebo, Michael). This was my first viewing and I was very impressed with what I saw. The four were in various stages of completion. The villa that Stephen and Michael lived in was complete and absolutely gorgeous right down to the swimming pool. The second was just a shell but we could see the potential. The concrete slabs had been poured for villa numbers three and four but nothing could be done until the almost complete one was sold.

I introduced all my new friends, including Raven, Cleo and her entourage to my old friends, Stephen and Michael. Our hosts were thrilled to meet up again with Chris and Margaret along with Brits Veronica and Ted and several couples who came out from Kalkan to see the property. We entertained ourselves while Stephen and Michael took care of business.

We spent the entire afternoon talking, laughing, eating, drinking and, of course, swimming in the pool that overlooked what the tourists called 'The Turquoise Coast' because of the aqua color of the water. The Greek and Turkish islands that dotted the seascape were close enough to see the vegetation-covered mounds that were set against a perfect light blue and cloudless sky. The view was breathtaking!

Although this was a very different trip from the first one, where everything appeared idyllic, my life finally seemed to be falling into place or falling apart, I'm not sure which.

Chapter 10

Down to Business

I was spending my days writing which delighted me. It was on this second trip that I realized why women have more than one child: they forget what pain is and I too had forgotten most of the pain of the previous trip.

The heat was as oppressive as it had been on the first go-round. This shouldn't have surprised me since I had returned at exactly the same time of year, but somehow I was stunned by it. Summers in Turkey, from beginning to end, are unbearably hot. That too I knew that from the first trip. On a day-to-day basis there is absolutely no let up from the soul-shriveling heat. Again, exactly like the first trip. There is never a cloud in the sky that would block out the sun for even a minute or two of blessed relief. That too I knew from the first trip.

For the second time, in as many years, I was in extreme pain due to the prevailing weather conditions. It is now forever etched in my brain, and will remain so on every hot sunny day, that "prickly heat" is an extremely painful medical condition.

Two weeks into my trip I had officially "missed" my flight back to Britain so come-what-may I had allowed myself to become "stuck" in Turkey. I decided to make the best use of my time. I would start by putting all my notes into some kind of writing order.

Yes, I was happy to be with my dear friends, despite their never ending money problems. Yes, I was happy to be in a place that was totally affordable and didn't really worry about the fact that I only had three thousand dollars in Canadian traveler's checks. Yes, I was happy to be making new acquaintances that seemed to amuse me for short periods of

131

time. In between all this 'happiness' I continued writing my book and did the best I could to try and keep my spirits up. It wasn't the least bit easy.

Stephen and Michael, despite the fact that they had been together for more years than any married couple I know, whether in Britain or in Turkey, were constantly snarling and biting at each other. They were amusing and very generous to their guests, as I had experienced, but they were not always pleasant to be around. I missed the "old" them.

Smiley, with his womanizing, was a constant hot topic of conversation within our group; but it was heartbreaking to talk to his wife who showed up occasionally with facial bruises and just wanted to talk. Without having anyone local to turn to she frequently latched on to me. This would not sit well with Smiley who would often "accidentally" bump into me as we passed. I also received the occasional punch in the back when he walked by my chair, but never at his establishment. I stayed away as much as possible but worried constantly about his wife.

More weeks went by. Even with all the depressing problems that pulled me in all directions I continued to write. Even without my computer, writing everything by hand, I made strong headway. When the first draft of my book was finished I desperately wanted and needed to type it into something more legible. Suzanne Swann heard about my predicament since I had blabbed to anyone who would listen.

She approached me one evening while I was out strolling down the main street. She was going to be in Istanbul for a week and was in desperate need of help in putting together some of her notes for a presentation. If I helped her, she would let me work in her apartment while she was gone. I was thrilled with her offer.

Within a matter of minutes, I learned how to operate her word processor since it seemed to be nothing more than a

Turkey in the Middle

glorified typewriter. By mid-morning, I had put her handwritten notes, which would have taken her several days to arrange and organize, in order. My hundred-word-per-minute typing skills completed the task relatively early the next morning.

She was delighted with my work and it was now time for her to keep her part of the bargain. We made an appointment to meet early afternoon the next day at her apartment. The morning coolness had vanished. Even with all the windows, front and balcony doors open, the place was like a kiln and I one of the pottery pieces being fired.

While we were setting up my own little workstation, sweat began streaming down my face. I mopped it up with my bare arm. I must have moaned because Suzanne turned to face me.

"Oh, I have a little trick for the heat," she said. She plunged a large towel into the kitchen sink that had been filled with cold water. She wrung it out, rolled it up and put it around my neck. "This is the way I work and I stay nice and cool," she said.

I thanked her, turned on the electric fan that was sitting idle on her desk and watched my manuscript and a few of her pages blow around the room like they wanted to dance naked in the breeze. Fortunately the pages, both hers and mine, were numbered. She laughed, turned off the fan while I sat down at the word processor and.....nothing. It didn't work. The plug was in but nothing happened until Suzanne showed me where to flip on the switch on the wall and then turn the word processor back on. I had only typed with it for her work but now I realized that I could proofread two lines of typing in the little box above the keys. Suzanne showed me a few other tricks associated with the machine, like lining up the sentences or backspacing the entire word rather than a letter because a 'w' took up more spaces than an 'i'. I hoped I would remember them all when I was on my own.

Her boyfriend, Mustafa, who runs the official Tourist Information Center around the corner from their apartment, would let me in around nine in the morning. He would then leave for work. I would have to finish before noon each day because the city power would be reduced and the word processor would slow to a snail's pace or stop altogether. The printer would not print in the afternoon.

For five solid days our arrangement worked like a charm. I started working around nine on that Monday morning and was done by eleven thirty or eleven forty-five each day. I always took a few minutes to clean up the area, put my manuscript in order and package it up to take it back to my room. Mustafa would arrive home at noon for lunch. I would let him in and leave. It could not have been a more perfect arrangement.

By the end of the week the typing work was complete. I had over a hundred and fifty pages of my words of wisdom. I could now start the editing process.

It was time to make up my mind whether I was going to leave or stay.

Chapter 11

Trapped

I wanted out. I wanted out badly and I definitely wanted out sooner rather than later but I had worked my little heart out and I wanted a little break first. I deserved a little break. I wanted to party and I was with a group that thoroughly enjoyed partying even more than I did! They did it often. They did it well. They threw caution to the wind and I was a welcomed part of the group.

On that first night out we went to Red Point, a bar on one of the side streets, and only three doors up from the main walking drag. It had a small dance floor and sweating, writhing bodies took up every inch of available space. It was the latest "in" spot. It was dark, the music was loud, and everyone that could hear the music, even if they were down on the main drag, was dancing. It was jam-packed with dancers, whether they had a partner or not. A couple of tiny tables hugged the wall outside, for those who couldn't take the heat inside. Most of the dancing, drinking, talking or gesturing spilled out onto the street and sidewalk

I was with my favorite dance partner, Stephen. There weren't many that could keep up to me on the dance floor (even if the dance floor was pavement) but Stephen was definitely one of them. When he wasn't actually dancing with someone he was swaying to the music. Everyone watched his bronze, hairless body with wide shoulders and slim hips writhe to the beat of the music blaring from the jukebox inside Red Point or from the music inside his own head.

Chasing the Lost Dream

Stephen and I danced the entire night away. I sat down with a thump, my hand over my heart. "Call the paramedics," I said to anyone in the group that would listen.

"Why," asked Ron, a Canadian whom I had met the day before, "do you need a new dance partner?"

I guess he had my number. We laughed, locked arms and left to have one last drink in a quiet outdoor bar. Like sonar we navigated directly to Café Corner for one last cool one before heading home. One turned into three both in time and drinks but we didn't care.

The next day, I awoke late, showered, dressed quickly and was out the door within an hour. I ran into Raven as I headed to my favorite breakfast stop. She informed me that she had purchased eight fabulous, handmade and vegetable dyed rugs that she was taking back to New Mexico with her and if her friends weren't interested in them she would keep them all. She was thrilled with her purchases and was absolutely positive that her friends would "go crazy over them." She had heard that the carpets from Konya had even better colors and were cheaper so she would be heading inland within a few days to buy more. She wasn't sure exactly when she was leaving but wanted one last swim in Stephen and Michael's fabulous pool. We met back at the coffee shop with our bathing suits within the hour.

We took a taxi out to the SEM Villas. The taxi driver made his way gingerly down the quarter-mile driveway hoping not to break an axle or flatten his tires along the boulder strewn one-lane drive.

"I wish they would get this road paved or something. Someone is going to do some serious damage to themselves or their vehicle," I said.

"The road to my house at the bottom of Baja, California makes this road look like a highway," said Raven.

Turkey in the Middle

"You've got to be kidding," I responded. "I guess I'll call from the last town and have you come pick me up."

"I could do that," she said. "I'm serious.....I would really like for you to come visit."

It was that afternoon in the pool when I announced that I too would be leaving soon. I couldn't stand the heat anymore. I couldn't stand all the fighting and bickering that was going on in town. All my friends were leaving to go elsewhere or home and I wanted out.

"We can't let you leave without a party," said Michael. "Next Saturday is the date," he said. "I'll make all the arrangements."

The next morning Stephen and Michael were at the in-town market and I went to the travel agency for a one-way ticket to England. Our little group met hours later at Café Corner. They had purchased all the food for the party while I learned that all the travel agencies were on strike. There wasn't a plane ticket to be had anywhere.

I wanted to cry. I wanted to spit. There wasn't enough liquid in my body for either. I had sweated it all out. Damn!

Chapter 12

An Outing with Friends

While I waited, moping for the most part, for something to happen in the travel industry, I ran into my Canadian friend, Ron. His wife Patty never felt well enough to go any distance from their room and the comforts of indoor plumbing, since some intestinal bug had attacked her, taken hold and not let go. Over a mid-morning breakfast we checked my guidebook for an interesting site, close enough for a day trip. It practically jumped off the page: we decided to spend the next day in Demre and Myra.

I learned from Michael, who had spent much time reading about his beloved adopted home, that St. Nicholas, although born in Patara, was the patron saint of virgins and became the much-loved Bishop of Demre and then Myra, now both fabulous archaeological sites. St. Nicholas, I learned through my Lonely Planet Guidebook, would drop coins down the chimney of poor unwed girls. The dowry would allow them to find husbands.

After breakfast the next morning, on the way to the bus stop, we ran into Cleo who, on the spur of the moment, decided to join us on our trek. It was a pleasant one-hour bus ride with lots of chitchat and a bit of sightseeing along the way, to Demre. Once we thanked our driver and got off the bus the sign pointing the way to St. Nicholas Church was close enough to reach out and touch or smack us in the face if were weren't careful. It was a very short walk.

We wandered around the inside of the crumbling building. Mounds of rubble lay where once a wall had stood. I took a few pictures leaning against a stone sarcophagus lying in

Turkey in the Middle

a carved out section of a wall and walked through a doorway with just the circular stone frame and nothing else standing. Between reading the description in my guidebook and checking out the site we were inside for close to an hour before heading into the garden. There we found a large blackened statue of St. Nicholas surrounded by children. The three of us sat on a stone bench looking around at the overgrown, dry, lifeless garden.

The walk to Myra was longer than the bus ride, and by the time we arrived we were hot, thirsty and ready for a break. We sat and enjoyed the lunch that had been packed for us at Café Corner, while sitting on the rocks that looked out over the Lycian rock tombs that comprised Myra. The tombs were five stories high and built right into the wall surface, like I had seen in so many other towns. These tombs were unusual because they started at ground level rather than halfway up a mountain.

Once rested we wandered among the hollowed-out tombs on the bottom row. I climbed up to the second-story ones to have a peek, but didn't dare go any higher since there was nothing to hold onto and it was a long way to fall. We spent most of the afternoon walking in and out and around a mountain filled with tombs. Except for the pop cans, cigarette butts, crumpled crisp bags and other bits and pieces of litter there was nothing inside the tombs, except for an overwhelming and pungent smell of urine.

We were back in Kaş by late afternoon starving and in desperate need of water. It was a day well spent.

The group, Ron, his wife Patty, Cleo and her friends along with others we had met on the walk up the hill assembled for late afternoon tea at Smiley's. Just as we were toasting our terrific day for the second time, the police arrived looking very serious indeed. It seems that another café owner had complained that Smiley's Restaurant was infringing on the sidewalk. Within minutes a fight broke out with fists flying in all directions. Smiley was held back by several of his friends but the fight continued with men (who had nothing to do with the original fight) throwing themselves into the mêlée, while the police tried to break it up and bring order back to the pedestrian area.

I couldn't help but wonder why Smiley beat up his lovely wife instead of the neighbor who constantly harassed him and caused him so much trouble. I guess his wife was closer and much less lightly to fight back.

With the free-for-all over, Smiley decided to treat everyone in the place to a glass of wine and a bunch of very sweet desserts. I didn't like him any better than I did before the fight, but I ate and drank anyway. I didn't worry about insulting him.....just my stomach.

Later that night I learned that two friendly Turks from our group were arrested for beating up the neighbor. I guess Smiley had more friends than brains!

Chapter 13

Food, Food and More Food

It might have been my imagination but I felt I was sliding downhill rapidly. Each day was more miserable than the previous one, as if that were possible. It was sheer torture. It was murderously hot and sweaty beyond anything I had ever experienced, even when compared to my last trip here. Oops! Am I giving my age away?

As I have stated more times than I care to admit, I wanted out. Sadly, I just couldn't get out; so I took one rotten day at a time. I bitched and moaned and complained to anyone who didn't move away from me when I was in one of those moods. I knew I would find a way out eventually, or the officials of the country would throw me out after my three-month visa expired, or it would gradually cool off and I wouldn't care if I got out or not. In the meantime, I partied.

The upcoming event was at Michael and Stephen's villa on the peninsula, or "Journalism Row" as it was called, because so many writers lived there. Everyone was invited. Guests arrived in packed-to-capacity taxies. The same taxies would drop off, head back to pick up more passengers, and return in record time. There were guests that I didn't recognize. There were some guests that Michael and Stephen didn't recognized. That didn't seem to matter as long as everyone had a good time. That was the Turkish way.

This event for me was a sad goodbye to Chris, Margaret, Karina and Emin. This was their last day and since they were packed and ready to go they stayed until after eight in the evening. Neil and Claire, son and daughter-in-law of Chris and Margaret, arrived late afternoon.

Chasing the Lost Dream

It seems that the party news continued to circulate around Kaş as guests were arriving well into the evening and long after most of the other guests had either gone home or were lounging sloppy-drunk anywhere they wanted.

At different times throughout the day and evening either Michael or Stephen could be found in the kitchen preparing fried string beans with almonds in olive oil or fried eggplants with onions or fried chickpeas in olive oil or refilling bowls of crisps or nuts or pretzels. I had also purchased some ingredients in town and decided to make one of my favorite recipes: sweet and sour meatballs.

With just one large pot and clean hands I went to work, after remembering to remove my rings and placing them in the corner of the kitchen counter where they would be safe. My fabulously simple but deliciously sweet and sour meatball recipe was prepared with my own two delicate, little hands; along with promises of cutting out of the tongue of anyone who gave away the recipe. Everyone who sampled my "jewel to the taste bud" asked for the recipe.

Michael apologized and said that he couldn't share it. "It is Joei's family recipe that was handed down from Aztec to Inca and I have been sworn to secrecy," he repeated over and over. (The fact that I am a Jewish girl from Montreal, Canada born to Romanian parents didn't seem to phase him.) They didn't believe me anyway when I finally spilled the beans.

Recipe: A thick layer of torn, bite-sized cabbage leaves at the bottom of the pot. A layer of apricot-sized meatballs prepared any way you like them. Another layer of torn cabbage. Another layer of meatballs and topped with a final layer of cabbage. Squeeze half a bottle of catsup over it, followed by any white soft drink, i.e. 7-Up or Bubble Up, diet or regular. (Do NOT roll or sprinkle meatballs in flour.) Bring the covered pot to a boil, cook for about 20 minutes and let sit.

Turkey in the Middle

Best served heated up the next day after it has been 'resting' in the refrigerator overnight. It can be served as an appetizer or main course. Does it get any easier than that?

The house was full on and off all day. Turkish, rock and roll, even some country and western music played softly in the living room. A few couples were dancing. People were standing around the kitchen talking and drinking wine. Some had brought their bathing suits and were lounging by the pool that overlooked the ocean. Some were talking. Some were sleeping. It seems that the world had slowed to a snail's pace.

A friend of Michael's was upstairs using the computer and sending out bunches of e-mails; one person, unbeknownst to either host, was on the telephone for hours making calls to friends in other countries. I was still there when the phone bill arrived. It was a shocker!

I don't know what time the party ended. The guests of honor, my real reason for being there, had left sometime after eight and I had wished them a fond farewell. It was at least three or four hours later that I zonked out on the couch, and no one had bothered to wake me up.

* * * *

The sun was high in the sky when I rolled off the couch to check on the coffee situation. None was made.

I washed my hands and face, swished some water around my mouth trying to dislodge the wee beasty that had used my mouth as a urinal and then as a mausoleum. It would definitely take more than water to freshen up my breath but I couldn't find anything else and I didn't want to go upstairs where the bedrooms and bathrooms were.

I opened and closed every cupboard until I found the coffee, the coffeepot and the sugar bowl, and went to work.

Chasing the Lost Dream

Fortunately, Michael heard my goings-on and came downstairs to make it properly.

There wasn't much food left in the house but a piece of toast along with the coffee was more than enough since it had been just a few hours before that we had eaten and drunk everything that didn't move. While the coffee was brewing I helped with the clean up which was mostly just throwing out empties. After coffee and toast I washed dishes while Michael dried and Stephen put away.

I got into a cab around one in the afternoon for the short drive back to the city, had some lunch at Café Corner and went back to my room for an hour-long nap while the sun was still blistering hot, nearly melting the pavement.

I met Stephen and Michael at Café Corner around dinnertime and we nibbled on mouth-scorching little pizzas, melon slices, chilled red grapes and whatever else they put before us on the table. By nine we were back at Red Point for a drink and an hour or two of dancing. It was the first (and last) cool evening that I could remember but we didn't stay long - we were all worn out from the evening before.

I met a young American couple while having breakfast the next morning so the time passed very pleasantly. They were far more interested in hearing about my adventures in Turkey, along with where to go and what to see then in sharing their own experiences; but they did slip in a bit of hurricane news about Florida.

I spent the afternoon at Stephen and Michael's along with Cleo, Thomas, Claire, Dorothy, Paul, and a Swedish couple I had never seen before. Her name was Ingrid and his was something weird like Mascot.....or perhaps that was his job on Ingrid's team, I'm not sure which. Anyway his name started with an M and we were, once again, enjoying Stephen and Michael's hospitality.

Turkey in the Middle

There were new people running in and out of my life on a one-week or two-week basis depending on how long their vacations were. It was all becoming a blur. My brain had turned to mush. I wasn't writing because I had finished the first draft and didn't want to do any serious editing without a computer. I wasn't reading. I wasn't thinking. I was drinking a bit too much and a bit too often. I was out dancing every night with friends and still had not come across a dance partner, gay or straight, better than Stephen. As a matter of fact, sitting here editing this book in rainy Vancouver, British Columbia, I'm starting to think that it was a pretty good life if only I could get used to the heat.

It was at a goodbye dinner with Cleo and her friends that Suzanne, my Canadian journalism friend, and her boyfriend Mustafa, came to join us. We walked up the hill to the top street, overlooking the city and the harbor, and went into the small, private Genç Club with its three or four tables, for coffee and drinks. Suzanne invited me to dinner at their apartment for the following evening.

The following morning I went back to my writing/editing ritual and was once again feeling useful by updating the notes in my daily diary for this second trip. Over a very late breakfast, Hazel a British woman living part time in Turkey and part time traveling into parts unknown, bored me to death with ranting and raving about her abusive boyfriend whom she loved and didn't want to leave. In listening to her I suddenly realized that that is how I must sound to others when I moaned continuously about the hellish heat that I nor anyone else could do anything about. I decided to stop it.

I met Neil, Claire and Michael for a cool refreshing drink of vişné (cherry juice) and soda, and that evening I enjoyed a wonderful lamb and rice dinner with Suzanne and Mustafa. I had hoped to say goodbye to Paul and Dorothy, who were heading back to England, but it was after one in the morning when I left my dinner companions for my walk home. After stopping and checking in at all our regular night spots I realized that I had missed them.

The next day I received an offer that got me thinking.

Chapter 14

Mustafa

I keep using the same names over and over, not because I can't think of any other Turkish names but I am using their real first names. It helps me because I can visualize them better but I hope it's not getting too confusing to you, the reader, but here goes.....

Mustafa was as big as a house. He towered over everyone I knew, and my outstretched arms wouldn't fit more than half way around his middle although that was a position that I had no desire to test. His size wasn't the only thing that made him stand out in a crowd: it was his laugh....big, booming and infectious. The only thing larger than his girth was his heart. No one wanted for anything when he was around.

Ufuk, which I was told means "horizon" in Turkish, was an average looking woman blending into any group without meaning to or without doing anything special to herself. She was about five foot five, slender, dark-haired, dark-eyed, soft spoken and married to the giant. Both spoke English well. Mustafa was born in the Black Sea area of Turkey and Ufuk was born on the Turkish side of Cyprus.

Mustafa and Ufuk, new to the area, were transferred to Kaş because of their ability to build up a happy and supportive clientele, while keeping their staff contented on a year round basis. They managed the hotel across the field and up the hill from Stephen and Michael. Although I had only met them a few times when they came into town to pick up groceries for the hotel I was invited to Mustafa's birthday party because of my friendship with their neighbors.

Chasing the Lost Dream

I arrived at the SEM (S for Stephen, M for Michael and E for the son-of-a-gun who squandered their money) villa early in the afternoon. I spent some time hugging an inflatable dolphin for support while floating in cool velvety heaven then lounging around the pool talking to anyone within earshot. There was time for a short nap in a breezy, upstairs bedroom before taking a warm refreshing shower in a bathroom where a simple shower curtain prevented everything in the vicinity from becoming soaked.

A shower curtain....such a simple and useful invention and yet something so foreign to the Turkish way of life. Unfortunately, the shower in my current bathroom or any other panysion bathroom where I had resided simply allowed the entire room, along with towels, clothes, toilet tissue and anything else inadvertently left behind, to get coated with a delicate spray from the nozzle. I can't tell you how many times I learned that lesson the hard way.

When we were all dressed in our finery we headed across the back lawn and up the more than forty stone steps to the lowest level where the hotel swimming pool was located. We walked up another ten stone steps to a lounge area - where the rooms stood facing the water and the distant islands. Another ten stone steps up and we were welcomed to the party.

There were just a few friends, lots of family, and thankfully some of them looked familiar. I was introduced to the rest who were eager to meet me, the American guest. A couple of men, much younger than me, shook my hand in both of theirs. I also got a kiss on both cheeks from everyone. I can't tell you how many times I was asked if there was room in my luggage for a stow-away when I was ready to head back to America. Even Mustafa asked but he was really kidding. There would not have been room for him if I was heading home containerized!

Turkey in the Middle

No, that is not the offer that had me thinking.....

The long table was set with a white tablecloth and delicate, deliciously-smelling flower petals were scattered on top. The plates were already stacked at one end of the table, some of them matched, most did not. Some of the glasses were proper wineglasses and when there weren't enough of them, water glasses were used. My glass was filled with red wine before rounds were completed. We were all standing around getting acquainted when the food arrived.

Platters of whole, baked fish, complete with glazed-over eyes in their head, crispy brown-skinned roasted chicken, and both barbecued and boiled vegetables started arriving. Salads, bits and bites of spicy vegetables in olive oil and some things that I didn't recognize just kept filling up the table. Wine in bottles and large carafes sat on the table to wash it all down, and just kept appearing. The empties were replaced even before I realized they were empty. We were there for hours.

When I felt that I couldn't eat another bite the dishes were cleared away and desserts, sweet and/or nutty, were put on the table in between large bowls of fruit and platters of different colored melon chunks and slices. When I couldn't actually eat anymore I just nibbled. When I couldn't nibble anymore I excused myself from the table. I took a little walk and ended up two levels below on a lounge chair by the pool.

Never had I seen such a sight! With no other light except for house lights two floors up, and the night as quiet as a tomb, I looked up at the stars.....billions and billions and billions of stars. I had heard about the Milky Way but never could I have imagined such heart-stopping beauty. I lay there wondering which one of those stars my husband was swinging on. I wanted to cry.

No one called. No one seemed to miss me so I just stayed there, looking up at the stars. Around two in the morning

Chasing the Lost Dream

my friends 'rolled' me down the hill. I stayed with Stephen and Michael that night. I had my own private bedroom and bathroom on the third floor.

I awoke around nine and could hear voices; Stephen and Michael were already up. The smell of coffee permeated the house and I sniffed my way down the stairs and into the kitchen.

"Mustafa and Ufuk really like you," said Michael. "They would like you to stay at their hotel. They will only charge you what you are paying in town. Their rooms are beautiful and in season they get lots of money for them."

"I'll have to think about that," I said. "This is a short but much-too-expensive drive from town and I love walking around in the evening and meeting all the new tourists. If the hotel were full of foreign guests I wouldn't hesitate. Thank Mustafa for me and I'll talk to him later."

The weather out on the peninsula always had a cooling breeze and would be so much more comfortable than the tiny closet I was staying in. I really had to consider it.

Yes, that was the offer that got me thinking.....

Chapter 15

Heating Up

I was wandering around Kaş before noon hoping I would come, right or wrong, to some conclusion. I ran into Neil and Claire having either a late breakfast or an early lunch at Café Corner, and who were supposed to be on a bus heading to Antalya. It required only a short explanation. They had been 'hijacked' when they returned from Stephen and Michael's (and Mustafa and Ufuk's) party and ended up drinking raki, a sweet licorice-tasting swill, at the only disco in town until after four in the morning. They would be leaving to go back to England before the end of the day but needed to get into shape for the long bus ride south. I ordered some coffee and sat with them. I told them about the offer I had from Mustafa.

"What are you going to do?" asked Claire.

"I don't know," I responded, a little whine creeping into my voice. "I can't stand the heat here and although I really like Stephen and Michael I can't deal with their constant drama and their ever present disastrous financial problems. I really wish they would sell out and go back to England where they belong; but you know them - they won't leave here."

In the end they had no advice for me. What could they say that hadn't already rolled around in my brain a million times in this effort to make up my mind?

We said our good-byes at the table around two in the afternoon. The bus would be leaving for Antalya around four and they still had the last bit of packing to do. Their plane to England would be leaving just before midnight. It would be a long, restless day for them and as much as I wanted out I didn't envy the long trip ahead for them.

Chasing the Lost Dream

I met someone new, Bonnie from New York, within minutes after Neil and Claire left the table. I ended up giving her a mini walking tour of the town and then having a long, conversation-filled dinner at Smiley's. When they needed the table for more customers Smiley told us to finish our drinks and leave. I stuck my tongue out at him and mumbled under my breath a vow never to return here, like I had done so often before. Bonnie could not believe what was happening. Nothing like this had ever happened to her in Turkey or anywhere else for that matter. I more or less explained the situation to her and also confided how sick to death I was of his downright meanness amongst all the other stuff with which I was downright sick to death. She seemed to accept my explanation. We downed the rest of our wine and left.

Bonnie and I returned to the scene of our meeting, our favorite coffee shop. We ran into Stephen and Michael, and Barbara, another recent arrival. In that split second I decided that I couldn't leave the hustle and bustle and constant turnover of tourists in Kaş for the lonely, albeit cooler and much more comfortable, existence of the Peninsula. I would be suicidal in an empty hotel, trapped like Jack Nicholson in the movie *The Shining*. No matter how much cooler and more comfortable the weather was a taxi ride away I wasn't about to jump from the frying pan right into the flaming barbecue pit. Nor would I be happy with spending five or six dollars each way for the three mile, five-minute taxi ride. Stephen and Michael thought nothing of taxiing back and forth several times a day after some con artist "friend" bilked them out of their car, but it definitely was not my style.

Over breakfast the next morning I had a heated argument with Apo, my cute and favorite waiter, who immediately argued back. My hard-boiled eggs were nearly raw inside; the white part was oozing and disgusting and I

Turkey in the Middle

couldn't eat them that way. He took them back but ignored me for way too long. When he brought over the second batch they were only a little more done and much more on one side of the egg than the other, like there had not been enough water to cover the entire eggs. I'm sure that if I had sent the eggs back a second time he would never have served me again. I suffered through it.

As I was about to leave Bonnie arrived, so I ordered more appletea as we chatted. Within minutes Stephen came around the corner and joined us. In the searing heat of the day, breakfast faded into lunch. Finally, we left the table mid-afternoon.

I walked back to my room and picked up my bathing suit and my huge orange wrap-around towel that Paul, my husband, had found on a beach in Mexico. He had used the towel for years before he died and I have used it since.

Stephen and I took a taxi back to his villa. The afternoon was glorious. I lounged in the swimming pool holding onto my pet plastic dolphin for dear life and looked out over the azure-blue water; I was cool for the first time that day.

Dinner at the hotel with just Stephen, Michael, Mustafa, Ufuk and myself was delicious and was comprised of platefuls of mezes (finger foods) such as fried eggplant with onion, zucchini stuffed with meat, hard-boiled (like they are supposed to be) eggs, a variety of salads and each of us with our own little crusty loaf of bread. I thanked Mustafa for the offer of a room but explained that I needed my evenings to be in town. He understood, or at least I hope he did.

I knew that things were not going well at the hotel; he needed guests and the head office kept threatening to ship him to a hotel that was even more remote than this one. I was to be his light at the end of the tunnel. I had to apologize again and again and he accepted but I knew he felt really disappointed.

Chasing the Lost Dream

I had been in Turkey for five weeks. I had wanted to get out of Turkey for four of those weeks and had been desperate for the last three of those weeks – but it was not to be. There was not a plane ticket to be sold in Turkey. Any departing tourists already had return flight tickets, which they had purchased with their original ticket.

My evenings of wandering around town had been pleasant enough, with new friends and acquaintances coming and going all the time. For the second time in the same month I got caught on the way back to my room with the fogging equipment truck that went up and down all the streets in an effort to eliminate the mosquitoes that plagued the area. On an evening soon after that incident, while having drinks with Stephen and Michael, I did not feel 'up to scratch.' I felt nauseous and immediately remembered inhaling the bug spray.

We spent that afternoon and early evening on the phone trying to get a plane ticket for me, with no luck. In between the outgoing calls to various travel agencies, a call came in from friends. They were having a party the next day and, in the true Turkish tradition, I was invited.

Stephen and Michael would pick me up at my pansyion. When they arrived I debated whether I should go - I still had a very queasy stomach. Stephen assured me that he would stop the car immediately if I got into trouble.

Against my better judgment I climbed into the front seat.

Chapter 16

Latoon

We headed back to the Bolel Hotel where Stephen, Michael and myself were once again guests of Mustafa and Ufuk for breakfast. I told them I was apprehensive about the two-hour drive to Latoon since, for the first time ever and after over a month in Turkey, I had developed a bit of a problem. For the lack of a better phrase and not knowing what the correct name for it is, we shall just refer to it kindly as the Turkey Trots, or as Mustafa suggested, Ataturk's Revenge. Take your pick.

We would be heading out in two separate vehicles. The hotel bus would be carrying about fifteen people, most of whom I had never met. The car would have the five of us. I chose the car since there would be fewer people to embarrass me if I suddenly had to yell "stop" at the top of my lungs. As much as I would have enjoyed the drive into the country during more settled times, the trip, most of it listening to my stomach rumble like a volcano ready to erupt, was endless. We had to make three stops and only one of them was at a proper rest area where I could use a proper, and I use that term loosely, toilet. Couldn't be helped. The car stopped quickly and whenever I needed it and every effort was made to find out-of-the-way bushes or boulders. Without ceremony I would leap from the car, slamming the door behind me. On all fours if necessary, I would scramble furiously out of sight while praying (a) to make it in time and (b) not to disturb a resting snake or gigantic spider that I had heard so much about and which would make (a) totally meaningless.

Chasing the Lost Dream

Despite the fact that the hotel bus inched its way up hills, stopping for groceries and wine along the way, they still beat us. When we finally arrived at our destination our host, Turgay, who had been advised of my delicate condition, approached me immediately. I was told that he had a gift for me that would put an end to my problem. He handed me a cork that he had cupped in both hands.

I held the gift with my thumb and forefinger, looking it over from all angles. I told him, if aimed in the right direction, this could be a formidable weapon. When it was translated, he roared with laughter. He knew he had met his match even if we didn't understand each other. It seems that my sense of humor had returned the instant I realized that proper facilities were within "running" distance, if you'll pardon the pun.

Eden Symphony was a cluster of homes with several small rooms for rent around the patio, hidden in a forest of tall, thin pine trees. A rope hammock strung between a couple of the trees swayed gently in the breeze. A bamboo bar with high stools was nestled in one corner and the group had assembled around it, each guest with a soft or hard drink, wine or beer in hand. A drink tasting very much like ginger ale was handed to me and it went down in one long swallow. It quickly alleviated my thirst and I asked for a refill, making sure that they didn't put any liquor into it. I had refused everything to eat or drink on the drive over. This was nectar of the gods! I took the refill to one of the rooms alongside the house and used one of the beds to relax on and recoup some of my strength. I fell asleep quickly and slept undisturbed for about a half-hour. When I rejoined the group around lunch time I was feeling a little closer to my old self.

Once the meal was over and everyone had eaten and drunk to their heart's content, myself included, my Turkey Trots returned with a vengeance. It was agreed that I should be given

Turkey in the Middle

the Turkish remedy.....a teaspoon of dry Turkish coffee grounds, washed down with lots of water, and then a couple of tablets of something I didn't recognize but didn't care, to settle my stomach. I felt that the cure might be worse than the sickness and was very surprised that the coffee was not bitter and went down much easier than I would have anticipated. I was then presented with a cup of Nescafé coffee sweetened with lots of sugar but no milk and told to drink.

In between bouts of Turkey Trot I felt remarkably well. I managed a little belly dancing that was taught by one of the younger men, line dancing that I taught with most of the guys falling in behind me, and free-for-all dancing where almost everyone was on the dance floor with or without partners.

By the end of the day I was prepared for the trip back to Kaş. Even though we didn't need to stop at all during the drive I was still relieved when I was back in my own room.

I slept soundly, woke up late and made my way into town for a stomach-soothing yogurt, honey and fruit breakfast. Bonnie arrived within minutes and ordered the same thing. We hadn't been talking long when Stephen arrived, sat down and ordered tea. Before he had taken a sip he invited us to an English Sunday lunch. Of course, we said "yes" rather enthusiastically. Bonnie and I finished breakfast, had a couple of cups of appletea and hopped into a taxi right after I returned from my room with bathing suit and towel in hand.

Lunch was gorgeous! It started with carrot and orange soup, which was a new taste sensation for me. The main course consisted of roast lamb, potatoes, peas, carrots, corn, pigs in a blanket and washed down with lots of ice-cold soft drinks. It ended, over an hour later, with the most wonderful creamy, melt-in-your-mouth summer pudding. My friends had done a spectacular job. It felt like a taste of home despite the fact that I had never eaten anything like this in my home.

Chasing the Lost Dream

We all went for a swim, relaxing and talking in the pool. We dried off quickly and each of us chose our favorite resting spot for a half-hour or so. Once refreshed, it took hours for us to clean up since every pot, pan, dish and utensil had been used in the preparation.

After we had fallen asleep on the floor totally exhausted from our day of eating, Bonnie and I managed to crawl into a taxi heading back to town.

The taxi driver, thinking we were new or possibly drunk tourists, hadn't put on the meter and tried to charge us four hundred thousand liras. I objected loudly and angrily, and he immediately brought the price down to the normal three hundred and fifty thousand, which even then was exorbitant since sixty thousand was equivalent to a Canadian dollar. From pickup to delivery was less than ten minutes if he stayed anywhere close to the speed limit.....which almost never happened. I always worried about those crazy drivers catapulting themselves, and me, off the cliff into the gorgeous turquoise water a hundred feet below.

When I arrived home all the lights in the building were out and I had to make my way up three flights of stairs in darkness. Fortunately each landing was open air and I could make out doorways by the moonlight. I found my room without much of a problem but couldn't help but wonder what was scurrying away underfoot as I stepped inside. I tried not to think about it.

I was jolted awake at around five in the morning to the sound of dogs barking, and upstairs neighbors thinking they were in a soccer stadium in the throws of an overtime game and having to talk above the din. This was the only comfortably cool portion of the day, when I was in my deepest sleep, free from dreams and nightmares and thoughts of wanting to run

Turkey in the Middle

away to another part of the world. I felt like screaming at the top of my lungs!

I did curse.....not loud enough and definitely not long enough.....but a curse is a curse.

Chapter 17

In Sickness.....

It didn't take much to ruin what might have been a perfectly acceptable day. Since the mid-summer's night 'screaming fest' I had spent almost a full week wandering around like a zombie. Despite my resolve to keep a smile on my face and the mumbling and grumbling to myself, I failed miserably. Since that middle-of-the-night fiasco I had complained so often about the heat that no one wanted to talk to me, and frankly, there were few people left in my Turkish life that I wanted to talk to anyway.

There still wasn't a plane ticket to be had in Kaş or in any of the towns around, and I didn't know what to do with myself. I was lounging around Café Corner late afternoon, allowing others in the group to lead the conversations and discussions, which was definitely unlike me. I didn't even realize that there were two new couples and several other new singles in the group; that was definitely a new low and desperate point for me.

Jean and Brian, very British indeed, owned a bar on the Isle of Wight and were in Turkey for some of the hot, balmy weather that had now driven me slightly over the brink of sanity (a very short trip for me). When they told me that it was the constant, cold drizzle of England that had caused them to turn the bar over to their manager in order to escape for a week of holidays, my spirits lifted slightly. I had totally forgotten what it felt like to be cold and I couldn't even remember the last time I had felt rain. I just knew that I wanted some of it.

Jim and Diane, both mid-forties, were from Philadelphia and I suddenly felt calm enough to enjoy listening to English

Turkey in the Middle

spoken as I knew it. Jim was a grade-school teacher and Diane was a lawyer.

Also new in the group were Lyla and Reynolds. They were traveling companions who had met at a small café in Istanbul on the second day of the trip. Both were Americans but she was of Iranian descent, and her beauty was the source of everyone's staring.

Laurel and Tim Pennick were on a three-month world tour and would be circling the globe before landing back in Arizona. They were in our area just overnight, heading to Antalya on the first bus out in the morning and then parts unknown.

Before the night was over we had talked our way well past midnight. We had eaten enough of whatever was put in the middle of our joined tables to not want another morsel of food for a day or more. We had drunk enough booze and soft drinks to guarantee a good night's sleep. When the talking was over we headed down the street where we danced at Red Point until I wondered if I could actually walk home. I don't think I got back to my room much before four in the morning.

My good humor was back, albeit temporarily.

The next morning I again walked over to the Bougainvillea Hotel as I had done every day to check on a possible plane ticket. And again, the manager suggested I come back the next day. That didn't happen. Life interfered.

I walked back to my breakfast spot where most of us had become fixtures. Stephen was already there waiting for me. "Something has happened to Mustafa," he said without preamble. "Ufuk has taken him to a hospital in Fethiye and they are on their way back home now. "Will you come back with me to the hotel?"

Chasing the Lost Dream

"Yes," I said, not feeling the urgency of rushing since Mustafa and Ufuk were not back yet, "but I need some coffee and breakfast. What happened?"

"Things are really going downhill at the hotel," said Stephen. "Mustafa received a call from head office last evening telling him that he has to get some customers in or they're moving him out to someplace even more remote. The bus boy dropped a whole tray full of dishes, smashing about a quarter of the supply. The kitchen help were yelling and swearing at each other. Mustafa suddenly screamed, clutched his head and slid down the wall. Ufuk took him to the hospital last night."

Stephen and I arrived just as Mustafa was settling into a lounge chair on the deck with the large dining table. Ufuk was in the kitchen preparing a light lunch for all of us. We talked for over an hour and my friend seemed to relax a little as he made jokes about his condition. He wasn't exactly pasty-white or ashen-looking but there was very little color in his normally tanned face. He was enjoying the sunshine, while the rest of us sat in the shady area of the patio.

When Mustafa went for a nap I helped Ufuk clean up and put the dishes in the sink. One of the young men washed them and we continued our conversation on the patio.

"They don't know what happened," she said suddenly feeling the strain of it all. "They gave him some tablets to relax and told him to take it easy and rest. They don't know him - he will never relax."

We talked for only a few more minutes and I suggested that she take a nap since everything was quiet and she would need her strength for whatever happened next. It was again too hot to really move around.

Stephen and I walked back across the field to his place. Michael was lounging in the living room and before we knew what was happening we were all asleep in front of the television

Turkey in the Middle

set. I took up residence on the couch. Michael curled up on a huge chair and Stephen was on the floor, his back leaning against huge, colorful hand-woven pillows. We slept soundly but not for long. After dinner we took a taxi back into town for more of what we did every night.

It was Stephen knocking on my door early the next morning. "Mustafa is worse," he said the minute I opened the door. "It took all of the young men working in the hotel to get him up off the floor where he collapsed. They put him to bed."

Both Stephen and Michael had stayed by Mustafa's bed most of the night and hadn't been to bed yet. Michael was there now and needed a break. Ufuk had been on the phone since it happened trying to find a doctor, a hospital that would accept him and an ambulance to get him to the hospital.

"Can you come?" he asked pleadingly, knowing full well that I would never say "no."

I dressed quickly and hopped into a cab heading out to the hotel. Ufuk, looking very pale, greeted me at the door with a kiss on both cheeks. Her dark eyes were filled with worry and sadness and fatigue. Michael too greeted me with a kiss on both cheeks, thanked me for coming, and then went home with Stephen.

Mustafa lay in bed wearing only his underpants. A damp cloth was draped over his head. He opened his eyes when I walked into the room and gave me a wan smile.

"How are you doing?" I asked not really expecting an answer.

"I'm okay," he said weakly.

"Would you like me to cool you off with a sponge and some water," to which he only nodded.

Within minutes, in a much stronger and huskier voice than I had heard since the start of the ordeal, he said, "give me the phone." He then told me what numbers to dial.

Chasing the Lost Dream

"Who are you calling?" I asked, a little annoyed that he felt well enough to call someone yet was lying there like a lump, being waited on hand and foot.

"None of your business," came his rude answer. "Michael," he said into the phone. "Yes, Joei is here now taking care of me. She's giving me a sponge bath and wants to take off my underpants but I won't let her. (Pause) I have heard that American women are desperate for sex but this is crazy. She knows that I am sick."

"Give me that," I said hardly able to contain my laughter as I grabbed the phone out of his hand. "Get some sleep, Michael."

While I stayed with Mustafa, Ufuk went into town to arrange for an ambulance. Money had to be withdrawn from the bank and payment guaranteed before the ambulance would be dispatched.

The ambulance arrived silently later in the day. That's when the rest of the nightmare played itself out. We all stood there watching, our mouths hanging open in disbelief.

We didn't know what to do or how to help.

Chapter 18

An Unhappy End

The ambulance parked on the road at the top of the hill. Two attendants with a stretcher between them made their way down the more than fifty stone steps to the bedroom where Mustafa lay unable to move. We could hear Mustafa moaning no matter how far away we stood.

The attendants took one look at the size of him and knew that the two of them could not do it by themselves. Two young men on the hotel staff were called in to help and the look on their faces told a story that didn't need words. With monumental effort Mustafa was rolled onto the litter. They had trouble getting him through the door with four pairs of hands, each pair clutching one side or end of the stretcher. By the time they were out of the room and on the patio all four were sweating under the enormous burden.

They made it a little more than a quarter of the way up the uneven stone steps but couldn't manage the rest of the way since they were stopping to catch their breath after each step.

Stephen, Michael, Ufuk and I watched in horror as Mustafa got off the stretcher and started to walk up the rest of the steps under his own power, with strong arms on both sides holding him up, the stretcher having been abandoned in the field beside the stairs. The two hotel employees supported his back so he wouldn't fall backwards which would have spelled instant doom. One of the drivers retrieved the stretcher after Mustafa and Ufuk were safely in the back of the ambulance. It sped away with lights flashing!

Chasing the Lost Dream

It was a twelve-hour ride to Ankara, the closest hospital with sufficient facilities to take care of a stroke victim. I never saw them again.

A lot of lives changed that day.....including mine. It made me even more desperate to leave Turkey, knowing that if something happened to me in Kaş help was non-existent. My family was a million miles away in one direction and the hospital was even farther away in the opposite direction. Although Stephen and Michael, their hearts as big as all outdoors, would do everything they could it still wouldn't be enough. Someone would have to be at my side every minute of the day.....feeding me, washing me and changing my clothes. If family or friends were not present to do these daily chores the cost of a hospital stay was astronomical, and then only the very minimum would be done. The whole idea terrified me.

NOTE: The rest of this story I learned through the grapevine. I later heard from friends that Mustafa had been in the hospital about three weeks before he passed away. Ufuk stayed in Ankara, too embarrassed to come back to Kaş because she owed Stephen and Michael a lot of money and didn't have it to repay. True friends that they were, they never would have asked her for it. They just wanted her back near them. I know they would have taken care of her, but she never returned.

*   *   *   *

I met Jan and Bectel at Smiley's. They were having a late, relaxing lunch complete with a carafe of red wine and smiled at me when I looked over at them. They motioned me to join them since we had seen each other a number of times before but had never spoken. They wanted to talk to a foreigner.

Jan, a Dutchman, was tall, slender and blond. Bectel, a native Turk and his girlfriend of many years, was dark-haired

166

Turkey in the Middle

and dark-eyed with an easy smile and an infectious laugh. Both spoke English with the accent of their country of origin. Since I had already eaten I joined them for tea and was delighted with the company.

They had heard about my predicament of trying to get out of the country and offered some help but not before inviting me to dinner. They supplied directions and an address to their apartment that was tucked away in the hills around Kaş. I arrived at five the next evening daring to hope that they could figure out a way of getting me out of Turkey without doing anything illegal or dangerous.

"What kind of music do you like?" asked Jan, the minute I walked in.

"I'll bet you never heard of it," I answered with a little laugh. "I love country and western."

We spent the entire evening listening to Willie Nelson, Waylon Jennings, Charlie Pride, Dolly Parton and others playing in the background while they gave me alternatives for getting out of Turkey and back up north. Had I not been so intent on ways of fleeing I would have been humming and singing along to the sounds that I loved.

Jan would be driving to Holland in a few days and I offered to pay all the gas if he could drive me to Budapest where I could get a train or a bus. He seemed embarrassed when he said he didn't have room for a passenger. Bectel told me in confidence later that evening that he usually slept in the car rather than pay the exorbitant price of a room. Despite my disappointment I thoroughly enjoyed the rest of the evening and tried to put my predicament in the back of my mind.

The next day at the Tourist Information Center I ran into Suzanne Swann and told her about my plans. She gave me more information than I wanted to know, since none of it was good news. A train left from Istanbul to Budapest every day at

Chasing the Lost Dream

six in the morning. I would need visas to get through Bulgaria and Romania. It would take a couple of days to get the visas in Istanbul. It was a twenty-seven hour train ride and the train no longer traveled through Yugoslavia. No food was sold on board so I would have to bring everything I wanted and needed with me for several days. It wore me out just listening to her.

The Tourist Information Center had a train schedule from 1993. Suzanne offered to call Istanbul for a new schedule and I could make up my mind at that time. The entire process was mind boggling.

I was confused with the instructions. I knew absolutely that I would get lost along the way, and in countries where they spoke less English than in Turkey.

What an unbelievable mess I had gotten myself into!

Chapter 19

Free At Last

I had somehow survived to the end of August. I moved in with Stephen and Michael, settling into the third floor bedroom, bathroom and balcony that faced out to sea. I had the entire floor to myself. I spent a short time every day walking around stark naked; it was heavenly. Occasionally, I went out on the balcony, knowing that I was completely away from staring eyes, draped my orange towel over a not-too-comfortable lounge chair, and read for an hour or so.

Friends came over every day for breakfast, lunch, brunch, snacks, drinks, dinner, to use the pool, or the phone or to play on the computer. One day it was Vim and Lola from Holland who came for lunch, stayed for drinks and swimming, and ended up eating dinner with us as well. Another day Michael and Dilek from Denmark arrived with Liam MacAuliffe (formerly from Ireland but living in Turkey for the last six year) in tow. Alcohol had taken its toll on Liam and he could no longer walk by himself. Even for the short time that I was in Turkey I saw an enormous difference in his appearance. The only good news was that he had finished the book he was writing and he was sure it would be published (posthumously, he joked). (Danish) Michael had admitted that he had seen Liam looking much worse, but was more worried this time because he had seen his friend this way too many times, and he knew that booze was an unforgiving master. They had arrived just to say "hello" and enjoy the sunshine but couldn't stay long. Michael was taking Liam to a doctor later in the day.

Friends filled the days, and evenings were spent on the phone trying to find one lonely, little plane ticket out. I heard

Chasing the Lost Dream

Michael's scream from the second floor while I was lounging on the main floor couch. "I got you a ticket," he shouted. "I got you a ticket," he yelled again but by that time I was half way up the stairs, adrenaline making the trip easy while taking three steps at a time.

"Do you have three tickets?" he asked, his fingers crossed and eyes closed in prayer. I could hear the excitement in his voice. In that split second we went from lounging around to whirlwind activity.

I don't know when it happened but Stephen and Michael decided that they too needed to get out of Turkey for a while. They were leaving with me. Michael called a taxi and within minutes of the phone call we were out the door and on our way to the Phallos Hotel to pay for and pick up our tickets.

By the time we returned home it was after nine at night. I hated calling Chris and Margaret Berry that late, now back home in Wales, but they were delighted to receive my call and assured me that they would pick me up at the airport in Manchester the next day.

We were up late packing, doing a little laundry, cleaning up the mess from our last dinner party, making sure everything around the pool had been stowed away, and all the other little bits and pieces that go along with a last-minute trip.

My personal packing was easy since I had literally lived out of my suitcase for the seven weeks, but thankfully it was over: I was getting out. I couldn't believe it; I was finally getting out!

I woke up singing. I didn't care that it was hotter than hell. I didn't care that I had to trudge down the stairs dragging my luggage because I couldn't lift it in the mind-numbing heat. I just plain didn't care. I was getting out and this was my last morning.

Turkey in the Middle

The taxi picked us up promptly at ten-thirty. He drove us to the bank in Kaş so Stephen and Michael could withdraw some money while I waited anxiously in the car hoping there wouldn't be a bank holdup or some other such nonsense. I was relieved when they came out smiling.

We weren't even out of town when we came within a hair's breadth of being wiped off the face of the earth by another car. I don't know whose fault it was but our driver was yelling at the other driver and the other driver was yelling back at us. Nothing was resolved. We just kept going.

I don't think I breathed for the four hours that it took us to get to Dalaman Airport. Stephen was sitting in the front seat and I think his eyes were glued shut and his face pinched tight in prayer. His fingers were clutched around a large glass "Turkish Eye" for protection.

My eyes were wide open glaring at the car three inches in front of us and whose tailpipe we could have smoked just by leaning forward. I was positive that we were all going to die and after seven torturous weeks in that country I didn't want it to be on their roads. I knew how inefficient they were and I feared that my family would never get my body back and that my private hell would be permanent.

When there was no car directly in front of us I was staring at the speedometer that registered one hundred and twenty kilometers per hour on the one-lane, part gravel/part pavement road. When the road opened up to two lanes I didn't dare look at the speedometer for fear that it was off the chart. I just didn't want to know.

Much to our amazement we arrived alive with all our parts intact. The airport was packed. I don't know how they managed to get so many people in one place without lying head-to-toe and vice versa like the occupants of a sardine can, but they did it.

Chasing the Lost Dream

We checked in immediately upon arrival. We boarded our flight within a half-hour. Our seats were in three different areas of the plane. I strapped myself in. The plane took off on time.

Between the guy in front of me putting his seat all the way back and the woman behind me digging her knees into the back of my upright seat I was not a happy flier. As soon as the "fasten your seat belt" sign went out I hopped out of my seat and wandered up and down the aisle. I found three vacant seats up front and plopped myself down in the middle one. I spread out and breathed a heavy sigh of relief.

I was free. It was cool enough to warrant a change from short sleeves to long but never dreaming that I would ever be comfortable again, I had packed all long sleeved tops.

This was as close to heaven as I got on my Turkish adventure.

Chapter 20

Dancing in the Streets

It was dark when we landed. I hadn't seen Stephen and Michael during the entire flight but I must confess that I hadn't looked very hard. I found them at the baggage claim and knew that they must have been sitting close by because Michael asked how I liked having all those seats to myself. I didn't feel an answer was warranted so I just smiled.

I grabbed jeans-blue soft-sided bag that I had checked, at the same time that they found their luggage. We went through customs very quickly and were out in the concourse of Manchester airport hoping to see a familiar face or two in the crowd. They hadn't arrived yet.

We sat waiting in the coffee shop. I nursed a cup of decaf coffee while Stephen and Michael sipped at the pints of dark ale that they had missed so much while in Turkey. Without ceremony I pulled out the wad of Turkish Lira from my belly bag and asked them if they still wanted to buy them, since they had said they would several times before the trip. Michael hemmed and hawed and stammered some unintelligible gobbledygook while Stephen looked stunned.....like he had just witnessed the second coming. I was a bit put out until I realized that they probably didn't have enough cash for the transaction or did not as yet want to think about heading back to their abusive adopted homeland.

I excused myself, went over to the Thomas Cook foreign currency window and exchanged the money, keeping some of the coins and a few paper bills as souvenirs. I had already decided that Michael and Stephen had been in Turkey too long and had become more than slightly addle-brained. I gave them

Chasing the Lost Dream

an understanding "eye" when I returned to the table and never mentioned it again. We weren't half way through our beverages when an arm went around my shoulder and I looked up into Margaret's face.

Margaret and Chris grabbed a couple of chairs from another table and joined us, both ordering coffees. My cup was re-filled, and we talked for over an hour. They wanted to catch up on the Turkish news from Stephen and Michael. They were delighted to hear that one of their villas had been sold despite the fact that there were so many expenses related to the sale that Stephen and Michael had ended up with nothing to show for it. They still needed to complete the construction and to sell the other two villas but had no money left. They tried to talk optimistically but were having trouble. They changed the subject.

At the end of our visit, Michael spoke solemnly to Chris and Margaret. "I'm turning our friend Joei over to you. You can inspect her to see that she is in good shape. She is now your responsibility so please take care of her."

I hugged and kissed them both goodbye, feeling very heavy-hearted. Somehow I felt that this would be our last meeting. "I really wish you would get yourselves out of Turkey and back home where they speak your language and do business fairly," I said looking from one to the other. "Turkey is killing your spirit." They just nodded "no," a sad, weak smile on both their faces. We parted, leaving the building in two different directions.

There was an icy-cold rain outside. I spread my arms up to heaven in the forty-five degree weather and did a little dance to the god of the menopausal woman everywhere. It was a seventy-degree drop in temperature for me that day and I could not remember the last time I felt so cool and comfortable, laughing as the droplets clung to my tee shirt and jeans.

Turkey in the Middle

Their home in Wrexham, Wales was a two-storey brick and, without the moon or street lamps I couldn't really make out what was planted in the front garden even after we opened the gate of the white picket fence. I was grateful to be inside. Each room on the ground floor was closed off from the other to keep the heat in. Chris escorted me to my bedroom on the second floor where I unceremoniously dropped my bag and knapsack. He then pointed out the bathroom at the end of the hallway.

While I was given the fifty-cent tour of the rest of the house tea was made and put on a tray with mugs and spoons, a bowl of sugar and a small pitcher of milk, along with a plate full of cookies. Margaret brought it into the lounge where the television was turned on and a fire was glowing in the hearth. We talked and reminisced until close to midnight. It took me that long to unwind from the flight and at least a couple of times each hour I remarked on how comfortable and relieved I was to be in the wonderful, cool temperature. I must have thanked them a dozen times.

Despite the exhaustion of the trip, the comfort of the bed, the layers of blankets and the coolness of the air I awoke at around three in the morning. I was freezing. I wrapped myself completely in all the blankets, yet was so cold that my teeth were chattering. I got up, found my sweatshirt and track pants, dressed, rolled myself back into the blankets and tried to sleep. I think it worked but I can't say for sure how long I lay there awake.

It was early morning when I opened the kitchen door to find Margaret making breakfast. She handed me a cup of hot tea and I wrapped both hands around the mug. We went into the lounge, the smallest room in the house. She wrapped me into a blanket and turned on a little space heater that blew warm air directly at me. I didn't move most of that first day. When

Chasing the Lost Dream

the space heater and the blankets didn't warm me up sufficiently Chris built another fire.

By mid afternoon the next day I suggested a walk just to move my stiffened joints and to acclimatize myself to the outside air. I put a few more layers of clothing on and Margaret and I took a stroll around the block. The sun was still out and should have been warm but it wasn't.

It helped just to get moving.

Chapter 21

With Friends

I stayed five days with Chris and Margaret, including the one that I spent wrapped in a blanket, sure that I was suffering from frostbite. By the second day I felt well enough and warm enough to go out visiting, and was glad that I had my bright red woolly jacket to wear over my sweatshirt that covered a long sleeved tee shirt.

Right after breakfast Chris drove us to Karina's house in Chester, a charming Welsh tourist town with two levels of stores in the business section that had to be approached through the archway of a magnificent stone watchtower. They had a town crier dressed in the traditional garb, and sporting a mutton-chop mustache and a beard, and at noon and four in the afternoon he announced the time and the news of the day.

While Chris and Karina did a few fix-it chores in Karina's home Margaret and I walked beside the river and through the park near the house. The park was spitting distance to the business section but we both preferred the quiet.

I didn't say much about my past except to tell Margaret that Paul, my late husband, and I had been to Chester a couple of times and had walked the park, in and out of every store on both tiers in town and the entire outside perimeter of the city. "Paul and I bought a couple of sandwiches and some fruit in the town center and brought it out here to eat." She let me reminisce a bit and said nothing while I told her a little more about my life of travel with Paul. If it was a story that I was repeating to her she didn't mention it; she let me talk. We walked back to Karina's when it started to sprinkle and made it back just before the rain starting coming down steadily.

177

Chasing the Lost Dream

We spent the rest of the day with Karina. We talked right through lunch. I wasn't the only one at the table that felt that our friend Stephen was far more feminine than any of the women sitting at the table. Over Chris's objections, Margaret just had to repeat the "Cappadocia Story." It was a repeat for everyone else, but new to me.

Margaret and Chris had gone to the most unique region in all of Turkey, the Cappadocia region with its underground cities, rock churches with mosaic-tiled walls, castles carved out of mountains and landscape more similar to the moon than earth, for the first time. They went with Stephen and Michael who had been there on several occasions, loved the area and knew hotel and pansyion owners or managers all over several of the small tourist towns. By the second day neither Margaret nor Michael felt up to snuff and decided to stay confined to their individual rooms. Chris went out to dinner and a bit of bar hopping with Stephen.

"Chris came home really early," said Margaret, "and when I asked him why he just shrugged."

"I felt better the next day and for the following two days Chris took me every place he had gone with Stephen. He was so afraid that people would think he was gay that he took me along to show me off. I never heard him repeat "this is my wife," so many times to so many different people in all of our married life."

Margaret, Karina and I roared with laughter before blushing Chris actually joined in and enjoyed the retelling of the story. We added a few Stephen and Michael stories of our own. I had to comment that Stephen was about the best dancer I had ever met, and I really didn't care what people thought because I would be leaving and would never see the people again.

Turkey in the Middle

While Karina put Emin to bed and fixed dinner for her husband who arrived home late from work, we watched a couple of short films, then drove home long after dark.

After breakfast the next morning Margaret and I made our way back into Chester on the bus. We visited many of the stores on both tiers, stopped into a little pub for lunch and by mid-afternoon were ready for a spot of tea and a buttered scone. We were back on the bus heading home to Wrexham in time to cook dinner. Coming and going I couldn't take my eyes off all the beautiful, old stone houses along the way.

Before the evening was over I called my friends Don and Marjorie Jones. They lived about thirty miles away and "would love a visit," said my friend Marjorie.

I fell asleep on the floor, wrapped in a blanket with the space heater blowing warm air at me, while letting the television set watch me. It felt like old times.

The news was on the radio when I stepped into the kitchen where Margaret was making breakfast. Prince Charles and Lady Diana had divorced, and when Chris arrived we got into a major discussion over the news. I felt that Charles was a scumbag who cheated on a royal beauty, while Chris felt that every royal male has had a mistress since the beginning of time and Lady Diana should have expected no less from Charles. We didn't keep up the conversation too long since the only opinions that mattered belonged to the ones getting the divorce. Lady Diana felt Charles was a scumbag and Prince Charles felt he was entitled to a mistress. What did our opinions matter?

On the last day with my friends Margaret had a few household chores to take care of, and preferred being alone to do them, so Chris took me for a ride up on the moors. The heather was in bloom and the smell was delicate yet intoxicating. I had been to the Scottish moors on a number of occasions but had never smelled the heather as strongly as I did

Chasing the Lost Dream

on this day. On a previous trip in lieu of the scent, I had purchased heather gem earrings for myself, and Paul had purchased a heart-shaped gemstone on a sterling silver chain for his mother.

From the grassland we drove out to World's End, maneuvering around the sheep that were standing stalk-still on the road, as if on our own little slalom course. We arrived home in time for dinner.

Chris and Margaret had to attend to a maiden aunt for the day so they drove me to Karina's. The weather was beautiful, warm and sunny so we spent part of the day walking on the path that surrounded the outer wall of the city of Chester. I could not believe how many people had crammed themselves inside the walls. We were back home around four in the afternoon.

Chris and Margaret arrived around six-thirty. We said our good byes right after dinner.

I would be leaving for Welshpool, Wales the next morning.

Chapter 22

Handed Over

I awoke to the smell of something heavenly. I dressed quickly, making enough noise so as not to scare the person responsible for the fabulous aroma. Chris was wearing an apron over his clothes. Every frying pan had something sumptuous cooking in it. Within minutes Chris and I sat down to a breakfast fit for royalty. My plate was filled with eggs fried in bacon fat, a rasher of bacon, a couple of link sausages, fried potato wedges and one of my favorites, thickly sliced tomatoes sautéed in butter. Not that I worried about it but I could actually feel my arteries being bogged down with a slow moving sludge.

"Where's Margaret?" I asked, in between bites.

"This is her morning to help out at the cancer charity shop," he said. "This is the morning I always prepare this exact same breakfast, and I enjoy it. Margaret won't eat it so it's nice having the company."

"Oh, my pleasure," I said, having just swallowed a mouthful of tomato that had scalded the roof of my mouth. "I'll eat almost anything as long as someone else prepares it."

We made short work of the breakfast although we did linger over the toast and a couple of cups of coffee. I helped with the dishes before heading back upstairs to shower, finish my packing, strip the bed and clean my room.

My bags were waiting at the front door while Chris washed and put away the coffee cups. We were out the door a little before noon, and had picked up Margaret at the shop before heading out for Welshpool. We stopped for a fish-and-chips lunch at a quaint little pub along the way.

Chasing the Lost Dream

I knocked on Don and Marjorie Jones's door. It was flung open by Marjorie and we were in a wrap-around hug and dancing before I even said hello. When the hullabaloo stopped I introduced Chris and Margaret.

"I'm turning our friend Joei over to you," Margaret said to Don. "You can inspect her to see that she is in good shape. She is now your responsibility so please take good care of her," said Margaret. The three of us had a good hearty laugh, and before we sat down I had to explain the joke to Marjorie and Don who had been looking at Margaret like she was a two-headed alien that had just invaded their home.

We had tea and biscuits. It was an hour or so later that we said goodbye to Chris and Margaret. Our conversation didn't suffer from the interruption, though as we yakked on like magpies.

The Joneses lived in a one-bedroom senior's apartment, in the heart of Welshpool. Since they knew I would be spending more than a day or two, I expected to be sleeping on a sofa-couch of some kind. That was not the case. The apartment building had several "guest rooms" that, for a very nominal fee, could be used for visitors. Thankfully I had called Marjorie early enough to rent one of those rooms for three days.

We went downstairs to the main floor and I put my luggage in the room. It was positively charming: it had an en suite bathroom, and the bed, a rather small double, was comfy to the touch, with a green and blue comforter that matched the curtains. The side table had a lamp for reading with a crocheted doily under the base. There were also several extra blankets neatly folded in the closet in case I needed them. I just dumped my luggage and went back upstairs to their apartment.

Marjorie and I went for a late afternoon stroll up and down some of the apartment-lined side streets. Don stayed home to cook dinner.

Turkey in the Middle

"Don looks a little frail," I said on our walk. "Is he all right?"

"Yes," she said. "He is a bit frail. We used to walk every night for at least half a mile or so but he doesn't anymore. He's afraid of falling so we stay close to home. The less he walks the more frail and frightened he is becoming. He still loves to cook though, so I let him."

Marjorie and I arrived home just as Neil, Marjorie's second son, was coming up the stairs. There was another round of hugs and animated conversation before we went inside.

Since it was such a fun topic we reminisced about our meeting so many years ago.

Chapter 23

Reminiscing

I smiled as I looked at the little group, Marjorie, Don and Neil, sitting around the kitchen table.

We had first met in 1989, in the very early days of my adventurous life with my husband. Paul and I had sold everything, including our home in downtown Toronto, in order to see the world like gypsies, with what little we owned tucked away in a cupboard or closet or under a seat.

We had been traveling in a small motorhome that we had purchased in England so we eventually got used to driving on the wrong side and shifting with the wrong hand while in the country. Things changed rapidly during our journey.

We had crossed the channel and were now traveling through France. I had already had several rude awakenings in this uncivilized country and I was not pleased about it. Finding public toilet facilities that consisted of porcelain footprints, a chain and a hole.....and what the heck was I supposed to do with that? Campground showers that were supposed to be either for men or for women, but the French didn't seem to understand that concept; I would frequently hear talking and laughing between a man and a woman coming from the stall next to mine. I don't consider myself a prude but how was I going to get out of there without running into a mixed, partially.....or perhaps totally.....naked crowd?

The day in question would have been another one of those learning experiences since it had been hours since we had found an open campground, and it was close to dark. Paul wanted to park in a town square or in the woods or some other

Turkey in the Middle

such nonsense. I wasn't ready for that and told him so at the high end of my vocal range. We kept going.

I had promised that this would be the last campground that we would check into before resorting to something that he preferred. We had seen the campground symbol just a block before the turn. We turned up the side street, my fingers crossed, my heart pounding in my chest. The gate was open - my sigh of relief was audible. There weren't many campers but it was indeed open.

I spotted the GB (Great Britain) sticker on a van that was parked close to the bathhouse. We pulled in beside it. Don was standing outside and as we parked our vehicle with CDN (Canadian) stickers all over the front and back bumper, Paul said, "do you mind if we park in your front yard?" Don immediately replied, "your day's driving is done. How about a brandy?" Could we have found a better spot? I don't think so. This was our first meeting with Don.

As we got out of our van to greet our new neighbor, the woman walked right past us, seemingly in a hurry for the bathroom. We had just said "hello" when she zipped by neither saying a word to us nor acknowledging our existence. This was our first meeting, if you can call it that, with Marjorie.

We took up Don's offer for a drink. Marjorie returned about ten minutes later and could not have been more hospitable. Paul accepted a beer and I had a glass of wine. Marjorie prepared a small tray with a variety of cheeses and crackers along with Planters nuts, sweet pickles, stuffed olives and some dried fruit pieces.

After nibbling on their treats I went to our camper and returned with a tin of sardines, some liver paté, turkey slices, crackers and a few cut up vegetables. It turned out to be our dinner, but we were so engrossed in conversation that we didn't notice.

Chasing the Lost Dream

It was that evening we learned that Marjorie was Welsh and Don was an American from California. She was 67 years old and he 69 years old and they had been married only one month. They had met in Spain, enjoyed a very short courtship, went back to Wales so Don could meet her two sons and were heading back to Albir, Spain to purchase an apartment.

The evening could not have been more pleasant and it lasted until well past midnight. Thankfully, it was a short way home and we could crawl there if necessary. That was the evening we discovered that if we were going out for an evening of drinking to make up the bed BEFORE we left.

Sleeping arrangements took a little preparation. We needed to use all the seats and cushions, placing them in various directions and positions after sliding both tables down the center to make a double bed. This wasn't easy, since we were novices at it, and then made much more difficult when lots of booze was introduced into the equation!

The sun was high in the sky when Paul flung the side door open. I was cooking breakfast. Don and Marjorie were sitting at the picnic table between our vehicles and greeted us with a cheery "hello." It was during our breakfast that we heard the real story.

Marjorie had not zipped past us on the way to the bathroom as we thought. She and Don had just had their first fight. She had gone to the phone to call her son, Neil, and tell him she was leaving Don and coming home. Neil wasn't home, and when she returned to the camper we were there. Being a lady she felt she had to be cordial. Being a good actress, we never knew until they told us about the argument.

Before we parted to go our separate ways, Marjorie invited us to their apartment in Albir, Spain for Christmas. We all enjoyed the retelling of the story of how we first met

Turkey in the Middle

Marjorie and Don. Neil had heard it a time or two before but never with most of the parties present.

After the dinner dishes had been cleared away Don, Marjorie, Neil and I sat at the table sipping our tea and enjoying more stories of our early days on the road. The sun had just gone down but no one felt tired. Neil, the only one who had to drive to get home, lived close by, and he loved our reminiscing, so we continued.....

It was the year after Paul had died that I had spent my summer on three archaeological digs in England and I was invited to the Barry Hotel in Barry, Wales (just south of Cardiff) to celebrate Marjorie's seventieth birthday. What a party that was!

I had arrived early in the day before any of the festivities had started. I checked in, relaxed for a while after my long drive from Bristol, then showered and headed downstairs. Marjorie greeted me with a hug and a kiss on the cheek; Don nodded and said hello rather meekly. He then took Marjorie aside and asked who I was. He had never seen me in anything but jeans or shorts and a tee shirt. He had certainly never seen me in makeup. He was stunned and finally came over and greeted me properly. (He threw "wow" into the conversation a few times and I really appreciated it coming from him). What a three-day event that turned out to be.

The reminiscing was fun but we had to catch up on the current news as well. Marjorie and Don now lived in a rented apartment for seniors in Welshpool. Neil had moved into the area as well. Don had financed a hairdressing business, insisting that he would like to see his money put to good use while he was still alive. Don and Neil had a love/love relationship and Neil was thrilled when Don formally adopted him. Neil was in his forties when the adoption took place.

Chasing the Lost Dream

Marjorie and Don were so wonderful to be around. I spent two days there and loved every minute of it. On the second day I was driven to Neil's home, a small two-storey brick in the heart of Welshpool and walking distance to his work.

Neil suggested that since I had several weeks left before returning to Canada why don't I visit Roy, a single friend of Marjorie's, still living in Albir. "It'll be a wonderful way to spend a couple of weeks and you remember Roy," he said, "from mum's seventieth?"

The fact that Roy had lost an arm in a traffic accident made him easy to remember.

Neil called Roy around noon. He was very enthused since he had often thought about traveling around Spain, his adopted homeland, and didn't want to do it alone. Neil promised to call him back later in the day so plans could be finalized. By late afternoon Roy had changed his mind and begged off.

"Don't worry," said Neil. "One door doesn't close that another door isn't slammed in your face." We grinned at each other, laughed and immediately changed the subject.

Marjorie and I went for a long, long walk, and returned in time for dinner and to watch Robin Hood with Kevin Costner.

After a healthy and relaxing breakfast with lively conversation Neil and his roommate/partner Ahmet picked me up. On the drive to Shrewsbury Neil and I had a long talk about Don, who really was not well. Everyone worried about Don but there was nothing to be done.

I kissed Neil goodbye at the bus station.

It was a local bus that took me from Shrewsbury to Birmingham in almost two hours. From Birmingham to Bristol it was another two hours on a National Express Bus; and then a

Turkey in the Middle

local bus dropped me off in Temple Cloud. I had called Bill and Jean from Bristol so Bill was waiting for me in his van at the little post office in Temple Cloud. Thankfully I didn't have to walk to the house dragging all my luggage.

Everyone was home. Bill and Jean, Barb and Glynn and Abbey, Barb and Glynn's daughter, were all there. There was a ton of mail for me. The date was September 2nd. My flight back to Canada was on October 6th.

I still had some time to kill!

Epilogue

Turkey in the Middle

Nearing the end of October of that year, I had been back in my condo in Florida for about two days when my phone rang. It was Neil. I was surprised and delighted and in that split second I knew why he was calling. "Oh my goodness," I said, "something's happened to Don."

"No," he said, his voice quivering, "it's my mother. They went to Spain to get away from the chill. As soon as they arrived Mum wasn't feeling well. Don took her to the doctor and while she was being examined she had a heart attack and died right on the table."

He cried. I cried along with him.

I had the pictures developed from my camera. There was a beautiful one of Marjorie and Neil standing in the doorway of Neil's new apartment. I packaged up a couple of them and sent them off to Don. I never heard back. I know in my heart that Don would not have lived long after Marjorie so I know they are together again.....and having fun.

I couldn't help but remember the suicide pact they always talked about. To this day, it brings a smile to my face. Don had to swear over and over that "should Marjorie go first he would not position himself and commit suicide in such a way as to bring shame and snickering to her family." He always agreed.....but there was that mischievous twinkle in his eye.....

* * * *

It wasn't long ago that I saw an ad in the newspaper from Dragoman Travel Agency. They would provide the best in Turkish tours through Fethiye, Kaş and the Turquoise Coast.

Turkey in the Middle

They had an e-mail address so I wrote hoping they could help me locate Michael and Stephen. They e-mailed me about three weeks later after checking with the local office. They thought my friends had returned to England.

*   *   *   *

Bill and Jean are doing wonderfully well at home in Temple Cloud, Bristol, England. They are not computer people so it is by snail mail that I hear from them, usually once during the year and always around Christmas time. They love reading about my adventures so they get one of the first books off the press. Occasionally I get e-mail from Jean, directed through one of their grandchildren. I am always thrilled and answer immediately.

*   *   *   *

This year we lost my school chum, my dear friend and sister-in-law Sandra after a very short illness. She put up a valiant fight but in the end the cancer won. We all miss her.

*   *   *   *

Even though the binding around the edges is gone completely; it is tattered and torn and has a hole in it big enough to put my fist through, I still love my orange bath towel that once belonged to Paul. It stayed in my camper until I brought it into my new condo. It might be time to keep it 'for my eyes only' because vaguely familiar acquaintances are offering to replace it. They have no idea how precious this towel is.....to me!

.

Chasing the Lost Dream

Digging In

Turkey in the Middle

Czeching Out

Chapter 1

Where To Go.....Next

It felt so good to be in the bosom of close friends; friends who wanted nothing more from me than to sit and talk until I had told them all of my travel adventures and heard all about their close-to-home trips. Friends who would relish in my excitement or sit quietly saying nothing at all - trusted friends.....

My last visit had been just a few months before.....just prior to leaving for my private, hotter-than-hell visit to Turkey. I was physically worn out and mentally.....well, let's not go there; so it felt good just to sit and talk, and more importantly, to continue to enjoy the cool refreshing weather that I had craved. I explained to my hosts about the never-ending blast furnace type of heat that I had endured in Turkey, but my discomfort seemed to roll off their backs. Bill and Jean, Barb and Glynn had been to Turkey several times in the last few years but never at the time of year that I had chosen to torture myself.....twice. They all felt that England in the late spring and summertime was superb, so why go elsewhere when the grass needed mowing, the vegetables needed planting, tender loving care and picking, and outdoor lounging on deck chairs was essential to a person's good health.

By the next day I was ready for some serious big-city trekking; so when Jean needed to pick up a prescription and do a little shopping we were off to Bristol. Even though I had only been back a day Jean didn't seem to mind that I wanted to go to a travel agency that had posted discount fares. I still had a month to kill before my return flight to Canada and I didn't want to be sitting around the house, although it would be more

Chasing the Lost Dream

than okay with her and Bill. In my absence they had redecorated the upstairs bedroom and constantly referred to it as "my" room.

After her chores we stopped in the mall for lunch. Jean is what I would refer to as a "cheap date." We picked up some freshly made cellophane-wrapped sandwiches and a couple of bowls of hot soup at the only shop selling ready-made stuff, and sat at one of the tables to discuss where my next trip should be. We never stopped jabbering at each other and when a napkin wiped away the last of the crumbs on my mouth and took a fast swipe at the table we headed into the travel agency that sported the widest array of discount flights pasted to their window. I assured Jean that we would stop for a cup of tea right after I found out where I really wanted to go for my last few weeks.

Colorful flyers offering cheap packaged deals to Majorca were plastered all over the windows and sandwich boards of several travel agencies in the mall. Upon closer inspection the same problem existed with Majorca that had occurred when I wanted to go on a packaged holiday to Cyprus. The price for double occupancy was cheap compared to the price for one, after you added in all the single supplements. In the end I knew I would be doing exactly the same thing that I had done for Cyprus - just buy a ticket and be on my way. Even though it was early September and Majorca would be a little cooler, the thought of possibly spending even one more day in unbearable heat made me cringe. I decided to think about it a while. We returned home for a lengthy discussion, with everyone at the dinner table offering his or her two cents. In the end, my options were still open for discussion. I still didn't have a clue where I wanted to go.

After dinner, and while it was still light, I took a sharp right outside the front door and walked further down East Court Road to a one-storey brick, ivy-covered cottage on the left just

Czeching Out

beyond the first curve. Some friends of Jean's, whom I had met a time or two, wanted to hear about my adventures. David (or Mouse as his friends called him) was waiting for me at the garden gate since Jean had called to let him know that I was on my way. I got a hug and a kiss on the cheek before he introduced me to his life-partner, Dal, an English-born Pakistani.

Before I sat down I was offered a glass of red wine and a tour of their cozy little home and garden which took just a few minutes. Except for the stone walkway to the front gate, surrounding the house was a rather overgrown patch with weedy-looking plants that I think of as 'typically' English. I was on my second glass before we parked ourselves into overstuffed seats. We talked like we had known each other all our lives, and told bawdy jokes like we were sailors on leave. It was pitch black by the time I left to head home.

Without benefit of a flashlight I walked up the middle of the road, afraid that I might fall into a ditch before finding Cloud Hill Farm. Thankfully all the outside lights were on and the front door was answered on the first knock. Over a steaming hot cup of tea we had our last discussion of the evening about my travel plans.

Jean and I watched *Jumangi* with Robin Williams and Bonnie Hunt in the morning, and drove into Wells for the afternoon. I had decided: I would be going to Prague by luxury coach.

I suddenly felt the thrill of the old days. I would get into Prague early in the day with plenty of time to find a place to stay. I would have an open return ticket.

My enthusiasm was back!

Chapter 2

Company

We watched several movies that evening. My day-long exuberance about my decision finally took its toll, as every ounce of energy dripped away like sap from a maple tree. I watched the beginning of each movie and I caught the end of each movie. What happened during the middle hour of each movie was anybody's guess! I was sound asleep during each one of them no matter how interesting the film or how hard I fought to stay awake. I lost every battle.

The next morning Jean and I drove the fifteen miles into Bath. It was while we were purchasing my ticket that Jean informed me that she had decided to come along to Prague, with possible side trips to Budapest and Warsaw.

"I've never been there," she said, "and I've always wanted to go."

"Won't Bill mind?" I asked.

"No," she answered. "We discussed it last night and he said, "go." Bill doesn't like to travel much anymore. He would rather stay home and relax and take care of his garden. He knows that there is so much out there that I still want to see."

"I don't know how long I'll be gone," I said.

"That's okay. I'll call him when I'm coming back," she said.

I was relieved and thrilled at the same time. I could not believe my good fortune in having such a friend. I would be traveling to a new country, something I had not anticipated when I left Canada. I could stay for as long as I wanted, as long as I didn't miss my return flight from England to Canada, and

Czeching Out

for the first time in far too many years I would have a marvelous, enthusiastic travel companion.

We picked up two open-ended tickets and were so limited as to the dates that we were positive that we had chosen the right mode of transportation. All buses leaving on Thursday, Friday, Saturday and Sunday were booked solid. We chose Monday. I was so excited I could hardly contain myself. I know that Jean was equally as excited, but in typical English fashion, refused to show it. We had the entire weekend to prepare.

It was still early in the day so, with bus tickets tucked away in purses, we wandered around the tourist area of Bath, a city that has welcomed visitors for over two thousand years. There were overflowing baskets filled with pink and white and red flowers, hanging on all the light standards. We watched mimes, dressed in white flowing togas and covered in gold paint standing perfectly still in front of the entrance to the baths of Bath, which they did often during tourist season but I never failed to stop and marvel.

We went into the ancient museum that had been refurbished since my last visit when I was there with Paul. The magnificent temple and baths, built around a natural hot spring which rises to forty-six degrees Celsius, flourished between the first and fifth centuries A.D.. The remains, housed in the Roman Bath museum, are remarkably complete and among the finest in Europe.

Jean and I entered the newly renovated tearoom and wandered around looking at the wall hangings because the tearoom would not be 'serving' until later in the day. We then descended into the bowels of the building to visit the old Roman baths and marveled at the large statues hovering over the long out-of-date and out-of-use bath area. I couldn't believe

Chasing the Lost Dream

that I had left my camera and roles of film at home collecting dust in the bottom of my suitcase.

We were home by late afternoon, watching the *X-Files* and preparing dinner. I had been invited to a small, intimate dinner party at Mouse and Dal's place but sometime during our wanderings it had been canceled because neither of them felt well and didn't want to pass along whatever they had. I ate with Jean and Bill.

The next day Jean and I returned to Bath for some 'touristy' things that could easily have been done the previous day had we not rushed back for my canceled dinner party. I brought my camera with me and took an entire role of pictures before heading home. We also bought a few essentials for our upcoming adventure, and starting laying out our clothes and packing the minute we arrived home. Before the sun went down Jean and I were walking along one of the side roads, picking black berries that grew so close to the road that we didn't have to step into the ditch to fill our plastic buckets.

Over dinner we talked excitedly about our trip. Stupidly, we had decided to wait until we arrived in Prague before purchasing an English guidebook; neither of us wanted to carry anything for any length of time unnecessarily.

Chapter 3

Mobile House of Horrors

Jean and I awoke early the next morning and huddled over a cup of tea and some buttered toast to perfect our game plan. We would each pack only one bag. I would use my soft-sided, jeans-blue bag that I strapped onto a mini-holder with wheels. When not in use I could pack the holder inside my luggage and take it out when we purchased more than we wished to carry. Jean would wear a full-sized backpack for the first time in her seventy years that she had borrowed from her downstairs neighbor.

When the rest of the household was up and about we had a leisurely breakfast with thick strips of bacon, and eggs fried in the inch of bacon fat that covered the bottom of the skillet. While Jean had another cup of tea I succumbed to a cup of my much-needed coffee. We showered, dressed and finished packing.

We made sure, while packing, that our mind's eye was not covered with rose-colored glasses because whatever we decided that we absolutely needed for this trip would be carried through villages, towns and cities in several countries. It either had to be totally functional for the entire journey or it was something to be used up and/or thrown away as we traipsed over, under, around and through every country we chose to visit.

We made a list of incidentals that only one of us would carry. Jean would carry the shampoo which we would both use, and hair spray, which I hadn't used since my big-hair, French roll days sometime during the nineteen sixties. I would carry note paper, a couple of pens and a blank ruled notebook just in

Chasing the Lost Dream

case I wanted to write a story or two along the way, and for Jean to send notes home. Since the days of traveling with my husband I never really got out of the habit of keeping a daily diary while on trips. We each carried our own toothpaste and toothbrush, bar of soap and face cloth.

By late afternoon we put our swollen bags in the campervan in anticipation of our getaway, and went back into the house for one last cup of tea and to say our good-byes to Barb and Glynn, the downstairs neighbors.

Before catching our bus at Victoria Station in downtown London, we had a five-hour motorhome ride because Bill insisted that he drive us to our bus stop. We both tried to object, but he wouldn't hear of it. I think he wanted to spend every last minute that he could with Jean. The trip was done in two short stages.

The first leg of our adventure, from Temple Cloud to Swindon, took place in late afternoon, the day before departure day. There was little traffic at that time of day, and since we were using mostly back roads, we made good time. We stayed overnight with their daughter Debra and her family, enjoying their hospitality. We relaxed and delighted in an evening of wine, lively conversation, and a bit of news on the telly. I ended a most enjoyable evening with a hot chocolate toddy before crawling into a single bed, usually occupied by daughter Colleen who was sleeping on the downstairs couch. While I tossed and turned in this unfamiliar bed, Bill and Jean slept comfortably and peacefully in their motorhome, parked right outside on the driveway.

The birds weren't even up when the alarm went off at around four-thirty in the morning. Jean made us all a little breakfast and some coffee while Bill and I scurried around, trying not to wake the entire household, and dressing as quietly as we could.

Czeching Out

Within half an hour we sneaked out of the house like a pack of thieves in the night into the typical British morning dampness. We drove into London while it was still dark, not saying much along the way, and were relieved that only the last half-hour of driving was in rush-hour traffic.

Bill parked in the off-loading zone until we got our bags into the depot and then left to find a more permanent spot to leave his van. At Victoria Station Jean and I had no trouble finding the bus going to Prague. At first sight.....and second and third sights I might add, I could not believe that I had committed myself, and my all-too-trusting friend Jean, to this mobile house of horrors voluntarily.

Upon closer inspection, both visual and tactile, we discovered that the seats were as hard as pews. They did not recline at all, and in true German tradition the seat part of the chair was so short and hit so far up my thigh.....zat you vill sit up straight!

All instincts screamed, "GET OUT OF HERE! SAVE YOURSELF!" BUT, we had just spent five hours on two different days getting to this final decisive moment. I stifled my instincts with a cup of coffee from a vending machine that had the lackluster appearance of a watered down beef bouillon cube. The flavor, or what there was of it, did not come close to satisfying my lust for caffeine. Jean and Bill hushed their need for self-preservation with a cup of tea.

I shook my head slowly from side to side. A soft, audible "oh yuk" escaped through my parted lips. We looked at each other, cursed, laughed, kissed Bill and finally climbed on board. Since the bus was already more than three-quarters occupied we scurried to the back and found several vacant seats that were side-by-side. We took them all and spread our stuff out on the seats that we did not need for sitting. We knew even

Chasing the Lost Dream

before the bus was out of the smoke-filled garage that the entire trip was going to be absolute misery.

To add to our discomfort there was no food, no coffee, no tea and no soft drinks on board which we had been promised. In simpler terms, if we didn't bring it with us we didn't have it. Fortunately, thanks to Jean's camping experience, and perhaps because she was more used to the lack of services or had a better understanding of the British word for 'luxury', we had enough food with us, junk and otherwise, to supply a starving army on maneuvers.

Jean had prepared the food because she felt it would cut down on expenses. She never dreamed that the food we had with us would have to carry two ravenous tourists through four countries.

We missed our usual hourly coffee and tea breaks. To make matters worse, if that were possible, the restaurants we stopped at would not accept English coin, so if we wanted coffee or tea or had to use their pay toilets we would have to exchange Sterling notes. In each case we would have to change at least a five-pound bank note into the currency of that country. Much to our annoyance, as if each country's economy was dependent upon our meager funds, the bus stopped often on our journey. We did not want to cash more than was necessary of our hard-earned money in France or in Belgium or in Germany. We waited, and would cash what we needed in the Czech Republic. It was a long, dry, thirsty trip except to stop for the very occasional cup of tea along with the necessity to stop and flush that same cup of tea.

True to the booking agent's word, however, there was a toilet on board that could be used only in case of an emergency. Emergency it would have to be since I don't know when it was last cleaned. It certainly had not been scrubbed anytime during the month that we were on board.

Czeching Out

Jean, much to my annoyance and it didn't take much to annoy me on this trip, had the ability to sleep anywhere, anytime, including on a hanger in the closet if it became necessary. Not me. When I wasn't trying to make myself comfortable sitting on the seat or the floor, or trying to lie on two seats or three seats or the floor, or generally twisting or contorting my body in a shape that it had no possible way of contorting into, I was writing a nasty letter to the bus company. I ended the letter by complimenting them on their ability to train their personnel to tell atrocious lies with such a straight face.

Another misery to be endured was that we left England in a sudden downpour that never stopped. Since the majority of the passengers were English, the rain made us all feel sorry to be leaving our warm, comfortable homes. Unfortunately, the stormy weather followed us through France and Belgium. Just about the time we felt we could enjoy a little sightseeing the rain stopped, night fell like someone had dropped a curtain and all the lights on the bus went out. Being a relatively experienced (and exhausted) traveler I made every effort to go out with the lights.

We arrived in Prague around seven-thirty the following morning. Michael Jackson's concert had closed the evening before. That was when we discovered that it was due to his concert that every seat on anything that moved was sold out that previous weekend. With so many foreigners in one small, newly emerged country I wondered if any of the hundred spires that Prague was famous for would still be standing.

"Oh my God," I said to Jean, wrinkling up my nose, horrified at the sudden realization. "We still have the return portion of our bus ticket!"

Chapter 4

Prague

Within minutes off the bus we each cashed a traveler's check at a local bank, having been warned against exchanging foreign currency with merchants, and making sure we had some small bills and a few coins for walking around money. We walked into a little café on one of the street corners. I had a cup of coffee with enough power in it to keep me afloat for the rest of the day and Jean had her first decent cup of tea since leaving home. Once fortified and rejuvenated we found the subway station and made our way to the museum stop in the heart of Old Town.

From the subway station we walked over to a long narrow alcove adjacent to the train station where, we were told, were billboards showing rooms for rent. We weren't the only ones standing around looking at the boards. Prices turned out to be a bit of a shocker. I had spent too much time in Turkey where decent-sized rooms with a private bath averaged six to nine dollars in a currency that I understood. By the time I had it figured out, I discovered that the cheapest we would be paying in Prague was over twenty dollars per night each, for a small shared room with bath and kitchen privileges.

Since we disembarked from our mobile house of horrors, needing a break from all forms of transportation, we decided to stay in the heart of the old town for a few days. We knew just by looking at a rudimentary map that we had picked up along the way that we could walk everywhere we needed to go. We assumed that the Town Square would be a marvelous place to spend our evenings, since the pamphlets (and map) we picked up at the Tourist Information Center spoke glowingly about Prague.

Czeching Out

Despite the fact that we took a bunch of addresses off the board, we took the first available room that we came upon while walking up one of the side streets. Our initial euphoria had worn off and we were totally crashed out from the endless, miserable bus ride. We were only about half way across the square and were already bitching and moaning about having to drag around our backbreaking (one) piece of luggage. After closer scrutiny, we realized that the city map we had in our brochure made little sense since we couldn't find any of the street names, although the spelling came close on a few of them. We were tired of looking!

The room was cool and bright, but small, with two single beds that looked incredibly inviting. Each bed had one rather faded blanket, one large pillow and, before allowing myself to relax I stripped back the cover to see (thankfully) spotlessly clean sheets.

There was nowhere to hang anything up. There wasn't a closet.....not even a bare hook on the wall. There wasn't even old bare nail screwed into the back of a door. There was no dresser, only one tiny night stand that separated the beds, with one drawer just below the top.

The room looked rather shabby and in need of a paint job but a huge window at the back of the room allowed in lots of light. It didn't look as though there would be enough lighting to read comfortably at night but for now it was bright. It was, after all, only noon.

The bathroom was across the hall. It had a bare bulb hanging from the ceiling in the center of the room. The tub was huge and I knew there would never be enough hot water to fill it. I pictured myself sitting in about an inch of tepid water, sponging myself off, but at that particular moment I really didn't care. This was Prague, and I would have to adjust like I had done in every other country that I had visited.

Chasing the Lost Dream

There was a large kitchen to the right of our bedroom. It was a room straight out of the fifties. The stove and refrigerator were small and round, and a dingy white as if they had been scrubbed with a harsh detergent too many times. The painted walls showed some cracks and small holes of missing plaster, but the room was spotlessly clean right down to the faded linoleum on the floor.

It was an older woman that rented us the room. She spoke almost no English and seemed overly suspicious of our every move. Grudgingly, she gave us a key to the apartment door and another to the front door of the building, while showing us on the clock when we had to be back in the house. She showed us how to lock the apartment door no matter what time we arrived.

Her bedroom/sitting room was right next to ours. We peeked in when we made some tea before heading back to our bedroom to take a long, much deserved nap. Her room was almost as shabby as ours and we both felt rather sorry for her. She obviously needed the money, since prices had skyrocketed due to the influx of tourists, but also resented having to take lodgers into her house. I'm sure she did not sleep through any night that included strangers right next door to her room, using her kitchen and steaming up her bathroom.

Jean and I talked quietly over our cup of tea and fell asleep practically mid-sentence once the tea was gone. We got up around two-thirty in the afternoon and were out the door within five minutes, ready to see the town. We walked and walked and walked, until around seven-thirty when we found a pub on a side street near our rooming apartment.

It was warm and cozy and inviting with a huge fireplace going full-blast at one end of the pub. The smell of the food was intoxicating. The meal of the night was some kind of fricassee, and at least three out of four at every table had a plate of it in

208

Czeching Out

front of them. Jean and I each ordered a beer, which is something I almost never do, but we were in a pub and I knew beer would be much easier to order than any kind of soft drink.

Jean drank about half the glass in one gulp and I sipped on mine, surprised at how sweet and delicious it tasted. I went for a gulp since it was the first thing I had had to drink since my afternoon tea break.

The meal arrived: chicken pieces still on the bone with fresh vegetables and potatoes smothered in a sweet sauce were served with a half loaf of bread to mop up whatever remained in the bottom of the bowl. The food went down so fast. I think we inhaled the meal rather than ate it, but we were ravenous from our many hours of wandering around. When our beer was gone we each ordered another and sat contentedly watching everyone in the pub while they ate.

By the time we left the pub it was dark and much colder than we expected. Even our sweatshirts with long-sleeved shirts under them were not enough to ward off the chill in the air. We walked back into the Town Square in the hopes of seeing lots of people milling around. The place was deserted.

We walked back to our apartment, delighted that we found it without any trouble. I had made a note of the address just in case we got lost. We were glad that we didn't need to ask directions because there would have been no one to ask. We opened the door as quietly as we could but our landlady was in the kitchen making tea and offered us some.

Over a steaming cup Jean and I talked until close to midnight.

Chapter 5

A Walking Town

We were back out on the streets after a morning cup of tea. We stopped for breakfast at an outdoor café and watched the busloads of tourists congregate in the Town Square. It was overcast but it was not supposed to rain.

From our vantage point, sipping a second hot and steaming cup, we had an extraordinary view of the Old Town Hall with a fifteenth century astronomical clock in the tower. Since our feet were still a little sore from the day before we sat and waited for the hour to strike ten, and would not have minded ordering a third cup had we known where every public bathroom was located. We watched the clock in awe as a procession of twelve apostles appeared in the upper part of the window while the medallions with signs of the zodiac went around in the lower part.

We didn't waste much time dawdling after viewing the clock because we knew that we would be back later in the day to see it again. While we had walked helter-skelter the day before we now intended to walk with a purpose. We crossed the world famous Charles Bridge that joined the two oldest parts of Prague, Old Town and Lesser Town. Every post on the bridge had a statue or a sculpture dating from the eighteenth century. We stopped to admire every one of them not letting the birdy poop or the birdy itself take away from the splendor.

By late afternoon we had toured the gothic cathedral of St. Vitus, the largest and most important temple is Prague. The coronations of Czech kings and queens took place in this cathedral. It was founded in the late ninth century and took nearly six centuries to build. The final stage of construction

Czeching Out

took place between eighteen seventy-three and nineteen twenty-nine.

It had turned into such a beautiful day with warm, comfortable temperatures and not a cloud in the sky that we spent much more time walking around the outside of the cathedral than the inside. We spent some time just sitting on a butt-numbing bench, admiring the magnificent gothic architecture and going over our pamphlets deciding where our next venture would be.

Fortunately we reviewed our pamphlets closely and went back inside St. Vitus to St. Wenceslas Chapel. The facing of the walls consisted of precious and semi precious stones and was decorated with paintings of the Passion cycle, part of the original fourteenth century decoration. There were also scenes from the life of St. Wenceslas forming another decorative band. We stared in awe.

The Czech crown jewels are deposited in a room in St. Wenceslas Chapel and, of course, there were guards surrounding the separate room where they are housed so we never got to see them. This was the first church where we had to pay an admission charge. Obviously we didn't look like we were ready to kneel down and pray.....hence the entrance fee.

We walked slowly back to the Charles Bridge. A group of eight musicians had gathered and were playing guitars, drums and violins. We became part of the small but growing group that were watching. If I hadn't decided to sit on the sidewalk with my back leaning against the opposite side of the bridge we would not have lasted too long. Jean decided to do the same and we sat there close to an hour before my behind went numb and I had to roll over on all fours before I could stand up. Fortunately no one was looking our way.

Well rested, we walked back into the Town Square. That was where we saw the first street sign with Franz Kafka's name on it. "Before I leave here," I said, "I really want to see where he is buried. We writers have to stick together."

"Okay," she replied.

That started a mystery that would not end until our last minutes in the Czech Republic!

Chapter 6

Window Shopping

Much to our pleasure, it was still only late afternoon and there were crowds of people milling around our familiar Town Square. Tourist buses lined the side streets, their drivers reading newspapers or magazines, waiting patiently for their passengers to return with bulging bags, colorfully-wrapped boxes and whatever other purchases they had made.

Elegant-looking drivers in horse-drawn carriages, holding reins that jingled with every move and displaying a whip more for show than for actually making the horse go faster, talked to potential customers as they passed. They hoped for that special couple or small group willing to dig deep into their pockets for a half-hour or an hour tour through the city.

Every shop was crowded. The more expensive the wares the more crowded the shop. Most tourists left with a box or a bag with a memento of their visit. Jean and I wandered into several of the stores looking into every glass-top case. Knowing we would have to carry around whatever we purchased in our already bursting-at-the-seams bag or knapsack we didn't feel it was worth adding a memento or two and especially not the glassware that I loved. The fabulous Bohemia hand-cut colored glass and crystal lured me from window to window like a fly fisherman lured his prey and I couldn't stop myself from drooling and making little whimpering noises, my nose pressed against every pane.

We went into every jewelry store along the way because Jean has a particular fondness for amber. I became fascinated as she pointed out the differences between the pieces she could afford and the pieces that were way out of her price range. She

Chasing the Lost Dream

eventually bought a large, oval stone rimmed with silver that she tracked down in a small shop on one of the side streets.

We went into a couple of bookstores hoping to find information about where Franz Kafka was buried. The clerk either didn't seem to have any idea where he was buried or she couldn't understand our question. It was at that exact moment that we realized that we should have purchased our English guidebook in England. The books we needed were about three times the price in Prague, and the guidebook that I preferred, The Lonely Planet Guide to the Czech Republic, was not available at all. We walked over to the Tourist Information Center just outside the Town Square and picked up a few more brochures with simple maps.

While in our favorite pub for our evening meal we checked the contents of the latest batch of pamphlets. Over dinner, a meat dish in a rich, smooth gravy sauce, we discussed the next day's possibilities. We checked our stash of funds. We had purposefully kept our Kroners to a minimum just in case we decided to head into Poland or Hungary at a moment's notice.

By the time dinner was over it was dark outside, and again much colder than we had anticipated, since the entire day had been sunny and warm without a cloud in the sky. Although I had a sweatshirt in my luggage, and not with me, we certainly were not prepared for this kind of bone-chilling cold. We practically ran back to our room. We donned a couple of layers of warm clothes and went back to the Town Square - we really didn't want to miss anything. Except for a few people walking swiftly across the Square it was empty. We went home.

We spent the rest of the evening drinking hot tea, catching up on the day's events, checking out Jean's latest gem and reading by the ten-watt bulb in the table lamp between our beds. Before I was ready to turn in I updated my notes.

Czeching Out

We were up and out early the next morning. We checked on the validity of our bus tickets and found out that the bus we needed ran three times a week, and everything could be arranged a day or two before leaving. We left the depot feeling confident.

From the bus depot we went to the train station. We checked the schedule for České Budějovice, about half-way to our 'must see' destination, Cheský Krumlov, and decided to leave the next day on the noon train. The trip would take almost three hours.

Since our feet were still sore from hitting the pavement the day before we decided to visit a local folk museum. There we spent four hours wandering among the local, hand-painted treasures and sitting down whenever we found seats (which wasn't nearly often enough.)

Late in the afternoon we ended up at McDonald's, coffee and ice cream for me and tea and ice cream for Jean. The ice cream was served in an edible cone dish. We loved it. Neither of us had ever seen a cone dish before and, sadly, I have never seen it since.

I reminisced about my brother Harry. He once told me that he would never go to any country that didn't have a McDonald's. As I had done before in other countries I took the tray cover before it could be ruined with coffee stains or, heaven forbid, ice cream dribbles, folded it neatly, and put it into my pouch. I took it home with me.

We limped back to Pivnice's for one last delicious treat, a mouth-watering beef stew dinner and a scrumptious cherry pastry dessert. We crawled back to our room. I spent the rest of the evening composing a birthday letter for Harry on the back of the McDonald's tray cover.

Chapter 7

On The Move

We were up early and dawdled over cleaning the room and packing, making sure that a sweatshirt had not been left under a blanket or a sock had not walked away under its own steam to hide with the dust bunnies under the bed.

We left the room around nine-thirty, after one last look around, and arrived at the train station in time for a one-hour wait. We boarded at twelve and were on our way by twelve fifteen. The trip was slow with many uninteresting stops at dilapidated stations, picking up a few interesting-looking people, but thankfully it was totally uneventful. We got off the train around three-thirty. While Jean watched the bags at the train station I walked across the street and booked a room at the Grand Hotel. Perhaps the name was apropos at one time but at this time it was long past its prime. There was nothing else close by and neither of us wished to drag our luggage down to the main part of town in the hopes of finding something more suitable.

I checked the room before paying for a night and was satisfied with the accommodations. The room was large and clean and comfortably warm with two double beds, a dresser, a clothes closet, a private shower and a small sink. A full, hot breakfast was included in the price. For the bad news, none of the rooms had an en suite toilet. The loo, as the Brits like to call it, was located right next door to our room and despite the convenience I hoped that we wouldn't be listening to the door opening and closing and the toilet flushing all night long.

I walked back across the road to retrieve our stuff and then had to wait for some fast moving traffic to go by before

Czeching Out

heading to the hotel. We dropped our unopened bags and went out for a walk before we tested the springs on the bed. We both knew that if we got too comfortable we wouldn't leave. It was really, really cold outside so we didn't wander far or for long. We did however find a bit of a shopping district before heading back.

We ate in the hotel restaurant. We each had half of a roasted chicken with all the fixin's: mashed potatoes with gravy, served exactly as it would have been in any American restaurant with the ladle making the indentation and the gravy looking like a little volcano ready to erupt. The sliced carrots mixed with peas were the vegetable du jour. It was not very imaginative but it all went down well. There was a square of something chocolate with nuts for dessert and our choice of coffee or tea to wash it all down. Although the food was reasonably good, and reasonably well presented, and reasonably priced we were the only ones having dinner there. I'm not even sure if there was anyone else in the hotel.

We hobbled back up to our room for a bit of reading, writing and checking the many brochures that we had picked up at the train station when we arrived.

My big toe was throbbing. I hoped that it was due to my shoes being too tight and not the emergence of gout or some other such nonsense. I soaked my feet and could actually hear my big toe go aaahhhh!!! I took a long, tepid shower and went to bed early.

We were up and out early and resented the sprinkling of an ice-cold rain. Despite the fact that it was a Saturday we found an open bank, near the hotel, and I cashed a hundred-dollar traveler's check. It was a relief to be solvent once again. We went back across the street to the train station, taking our life in our hands crossing the busy road in the middle of the block, to check on tickets to Budapest.

Chasing the Lost Dream

We learned that a return ticket would cost about a hundred dollars, would take around seven hours each way and would deliver us back to Prague at around midnight. We decided to wait until after we had seen more of the Czech Republic before making up our minds about traveling to Hungary. The icy cold weather was starting to have its effects on us. We both wished we had chosen someplace a little warmer.

Once we found the Town Square, we took an hour to wander through a free folk museum, more for the warmth than the artifacts, and then up and down some of the small side streets checking out the simple but rather shabby architecture. We had dinner at a Mexican restaurant, with tacos, refried beans and enchiladas that were surprisingly tasty and very authentic-looking. Several different English newspapers were scattered about on most of the tables. We each took a paper and scanned for anything of interest.

We wandered home around seven after stopping at the local McDonald's for an ice cream, edible dish not included. When it comes to ice cream, weather is never a factor.

The hotel bed was very comfortable, and with breakfast thrown in for good measure it was quite the bargain. We were delighted to learn on our fact finding mission that České Budějovice is where Budweiser beer is brewed while Pilsen, one of the cities we passed somewhere along the way, is where Pilsner beer is brewed. This new-found knowledge made me wish I was more of a beer drinker; either that or I should head back to wine country where I belonged!

In the hotel lobby the next morning we ran into Susan and Melody, two young women whom we had met on the bus from London. Jean and I learned that we had missed a lively concert in the Town Square the night before. It could not have been helped. It was so cold and damp we felt that it might snow

Czeching Out

before we got back to the hotel and neither one of us had clothes for that. We were in no way, shape or form prepared for the nastiness of the weather.

Thankfully the hotel was well heated, but on that last night we didn't sleep well. Although we were on the second floor and it was raining outside we could hear teenagers laughing and screaming right under our window.

We were ready to be on our way early the next morning!

Chapter 8

Ĉeský Krumlov

By the time we arrived in Český Krumlov the sun was shining and it had warmed up to the point of needing to strip off our sweatshirts. Thankfully it was a short walk up the first side street that we came to where there was a sandwich board sign at the corner. The sign indicated that a warm and cozy, family-run bed-and-breakfast spot was just about halfway up the block with a similar board sitting on their front stoop. We were greeted with a warm, friendly smile from the lady of the house and a door that opened a little wider so we could step inside.

After a friendly chat and a cup of tea with the middle-aged, short, round, neatly coifed female owner of the house, we settled into our large, comfortable room with two double beds that were covered with handmade quilts. Gilda's English was perfect as she explained in infinite detail the places we might want to explore, all of them within walking distance.

We learned more than we wanted to know about the history and geography of Ĉhesky Krumlov. The name of the town came from the German Krumben Ouwe, meaning crooked shaped meadow, and although the town seemed to be out of the way it was actually situated on the main trade route between Bavaria and Italy. It sits by the River Vltava in south Bavaria, and has the second biggest castle in Bohemia, easily recognizable by its 'Red Gate.' It is comprised of more than forty buildings, five courtyards and several parks, and took six centuries to finish all the works.

Gilda would have gone on and on and on but we excused ourselves so we could actually see the places that she had so highly recommended.

Czeching Out

We unpacked a few things onto the beds. I found my camera wrapped up in my comfy track suit. Jean had her camera in her purse with enough film to cover an unexpected coronation. We were off exploring after a quick wave to our overly- friendly owner.

We found the main tourist and shopping street just where Gilda had said it would be, as well as the old castle that had been recommended. The castle had a colorful craft exhibition going on in two enormous rooms on the main floor. The hand-painted, free-form pottery, the giant ornate picture frames, and the kitchen utensils were big and awkward and clunky-looking. Nothing in that room looked like it would have even chipped if dropped out of a third-storey window.

Everywhere we looked, and we scanned the entire room before entering, there was something unique to see. There were old, faded mirrors hanging on the walls in brilliant sun yellow or fire engine red or chartreuse green frames. There was fireplace equipment made of wrought iron that would need two hands to lift. There were huge desks more suitable for a warehouse office than a home, and tables that could easily seat an entire family.....and I mean immediate family as well as distant relatives dating back to The Great Flood. The chairs were so large and unattractive and covered in such hideous fabrics that we won't go into any further description. Neither Jean nor myself could imagine what the enormous room was used for before this horrible collection took up residency, a collection that would probably be here until the next fire.

The second room was filled with pictures and portraits done in muted tones. The faces on the canvases could easily have been used to haunt houses. We didn't last long in this second room and returned to room number one to see if we had missed a treasure or two hidden by the junk.

Chasing the Lost Dream

The exhibition was nothing to write home about, and good for a laugh, but the castle was definitely worth another look and perhaps that is what we were supposed to see. We walked around the outside of the building and were very impressed: it was a fortress, with wall five feet thick.

From the castle we walked to the museum. The museum was small with many photos of the village of Český Krumlov in the early years; it didn't take us long to see the entire collection spending a moment or two in front of each one.

It was still warm when we left the museum, so we preferred walking around outside. The cobblestone streets were filled with small gift and candle shops, grocery stores and a few outdoor vendors peddling their wares.

We found a neat little pub for dinner and washed down our meat stew with a local beer. Dinner was followed by a scrumptious praline sundae. It was dark by the time we left the pub but Jean really wanted to call her husband. We went looking for a pay phone. There were two well-lit booths side-by-side but neither one had a privacy door, so while Jean used one I took out the phone book, placed it on my knee and was hunched over reading it in the other booth.

It was the oddest sensation. I couldn't believe that someone was actually poking me in the rear end. I was almost afraid to look. I couldn't believe what I was feeling and decided that it must be some mistake. I didn't straighten up but turned my head around slowly over my shoulder, hoping that it wasn't some uncouth boor that I would have to fight off to retain my honor. I was suddenly hazel eyeball to blue eyeball with a giant harlequin Great Dane that a woman, about half my size, was trying to pull away from me. I straightened up. The poor, embarrassed woman could not have been more apologetic. I started to laugh. I petted the huge beast, whose head was well above my waist and who now wanted to lick my face. I didn't

Czeching Out

allow him that privilege since I knew where his giant nose had been just moments before. He leaned the whole mid-section of his body against me, enjoying the attention, during the entire length of Jean's telephone call.

Bill sent his regards and was delighted that we were having a great time.

Chapter 9

A Fellow Traveler

We were invited to a sit-down breakfast with Gilda and her husband, Willem. The table was laid out with soft, home-baked buns, butter and jam, and my much-needed cup of coffee. This was poured into the largest mug they owned as if she knew that I wouldn't be able to talk straight without it. Their kitchen was old-fashioned with lots of sky-blue cupboards and trim that was painted a blinding white. It was warm from all the baking and smelled heavenly. The round table was covered with a deep blue, hand-stitched cloth, and a matching pillow covered each chair. It was so warm and cozy that there was almost an audible sigh as we sat down. We dared not sit too long. We knew that if we didn't head out the door right after our eggs and sausages we would be content to sit there and talk to our landlords all day.

After all our travels, they were the friendliest people we had come across during our entire stay in the Czech Republic. They were not frightened of all the changes taking place in their country, and seemed to really enjoy having guests in their home. Perhaps it was because there were two of them, or the fact that they spoke English better than most; Jean and I welcomed their hospitality.

As it was, we were well into the morning before we moved along. We had talked for well over an hour, telling them about our adventures from the day before, including getting an up-close and far too personal sniff from a giant dog. They loved our stories and begged us to continue. We promised we would be home early enough for a cup of tea and more conversation.

Czeching Out

We were almost ready for lunch when we headed out the door for the Ceramic Museum. We both felt we wanted a little touring before stuffing our faces for the second time that day, so we walked to the museum. We walked a little faster than the day before because of the chill in the air.

Not only were some of the furniture pieces unique at this museum, but the knots in the wood were the center of attention rather than a mistake to be hidden. The desks and tables of all different shapes and sizes were fabulous, and we walked around for a couple of hours looking for the so-called flaws in each piece.

The next exhibit was held in two rooms of a church built in seventeen sixty-three. The main room was painted in an easy-on-the-eyes pink and the only the huge fireplace with an ornate mantel that took up most of one wall was of any interest.

We again visited several parts of the castle for the art festival and walked up the one hundred and sixty-one steps to the top of the tower for the usual reasons; the exercise and the view. We walked the gardens, definitely not at their peak, and saw the revolving stage, where plays would have been performed during better weather. Unfortunately it was much too cold to be working, and there were only a few others walking around outside.

We were beginning to know this town, lying on the foothills of the Šumava Mountains, like the back of our hands.....varicose veins and all. We decided that if our next door neighbors at the bed-and-breakfast arrived home early enough we would check their English guidebook to make sure we had seen all we wanted before heading back to Prague for more day-tripping.

We hated to admit it and definitely hated to complain out loud about it, but we were both very cold, despite the fact that the sun came out from under the clouds most days. We couldn't seem to warm up, and no matter what we wore or how many layers we had on, it simply was never enough. Except for brief periods the days always seemed to be overcast and drizzling or on the verge of drizzling. The evenings were a shade above frosty and we hated being out in them.

We woke up early the next morning, knowing that we had seen everything that the guidebook recommended, and headed for the bus station. We were still waiting for the bus to take us to the train when we met Ken Fischer, a rather attractive, boyish-looking, forty-something year old Australian who was also heading to Prague. We three took up all the seats at the back of the bus for the short ride to the train station.

Once aboard the train we were chatting like we had known each other forever, sitting facing each other with our luggage stacked on the spare seat. Then our train stopped in the middle of an empty field and didn't seem to want to move. A bus rolled up a few minutes later and stopped in front of our group. We all transferred off the train and onto the bus that returned us to České Budějovice. The bus dropped us off at the train station, right across from the familiar Grand Hotel.

We took turns watching the luggage while the other two were using the restroom. It was at that moment that I realized how much easier it was traveling with a companion. While that thought popped into my mind Ken vocalized the exact same opinion, and Jean returned in time for the discussion. Jean had never traveled alone so she contributed nothing to the chitterchatter on the subject, and eventually ignored us as we went on and on and on.

With Ken, our interesting traveling companion, we made our way back to Prague. Hana, hoping to drum up some business for the hotel he worked for, greeted us like long, lost relatives, at the train station. He led us back to Staroměstské Náměstí, the official name of the Old Town Square of Prague, our old stomping grounds. The room he found for us was a bit too far from the Square but so peaceful and quiet. We booked in for four days. Ken decided to head out on his own so we said goodbye at the door.

We decided that we would stay longer if the weather held out. The day we arrived was beautiful and we were hoping for more of the same.

Chapter 10

Familiar Territory

We started our last Friday by heading down to the train station. The train took us to the main bus depot. We accomplished our mission within minutes of arriving: reservations on the bus heading back to London on the following Monday.

Over coffee and tea we reviewed pamphlets, brochures and our notes, and determined that among the few things we still had left to see Franz Kafka's grave remained a top priority.....and an elusive mystery. We had followed the directions that various, supposedly knowledgeable people had given us and every one of those directions had lead to utter disappointment. We knew the guy was buried someplace because we had not seen him walking around the Town Square, nor had we seen signs that said, "Franz Kafka has left the building." Where he was buried was a total mystery.....even, it seems, to the residents of Prague. Temporarily, because we had to, we put our "dead author hunt" on the back burner.

We checked on a bus and then on the train going to Katna Hora, a picturesque medieval town about sixty kilometers east of Prague. The original source of the town's beauty and riches was silver ore mining, one of the richest deposits in Europe. Much to our frustration, we couldn't even find a listing on the big board at the train station. We were either looking for a different spelling from the one listed in the brochure and were not pronouncing the name properly when we asked a uniformed person, or like Franz Kafka's grave, it would become another never-to-be-seen mystery. To ease our frustration we decided

Czeching Out

the town closed when the mine did and they left the name in brochures as a tease to the tourist.

We spent part of the day wandering up and down some of the shop-lined lanes that we hadn't seen before in this old part of Prague, and found the most incredible bank. I think it started out as a museum with fabulous floor-to-ceiling murals on all the walls. We found the Powder Bridge, one of the entrances to Prague Castle, on our walk. We also discovered that once we got our bearings it was easy to find our way around town. We even found an all-English bookstore on one of the side streets.

Off the beaten track we found more (and tiny) stores jammed onto every side street and alleyway. Even though Jean had already purchased one piece of amber we continued to hit every jewelry store, no matter how small, because of her addiction. It took hours before making our way back to the Town Square.

Prague was jam-packed with tourists and many different languages were represented. During the day the Town Square was buzzing with activity. At night it was as quiet as a tomb.

After one absolutely gorgeous, warm and sunny day and one cool but still comfortable day the rain returned. Our room was extremely cold with only thin blankets for cover. We decided that we had made the correct decision about leaving on the following Monday. We agreed that we didn't mind dressing in layers for whatever the weather brought during the day but we were getting sick and tired of dressing in layers to sleep. Trying to toss and turn, wearing everything we had in our luggage was more than just a nuisance - it was exhausting.

The next morning, much earlier than we would normally have gotten up, we again made our way to the train station. After checking a rudimentary map of the country that we had acquired at a travel agency that specialized in local day trips, we

Chasing the Lost Dream

hopped on the train heading to Kolm. In Kolm, after only a short wait, we changed trains. We got off in Kutna Hora and nobody could have been prouder of our accomplishments, and without benefit of speaking the language.

Before heading towards the cathedral we stopped at a cozy little diner. It was not even the size of a one-family house and we would have missed it entirely had it not been for the aroma that made Jean's stomach growl loud enough for me to think we were being stalked by some enormous pussycat.

The azure blue print curtains on the windows and matching table clothes were charming and we noticed them only after a full egg and potato, toast and coffee breakfast with a second cup of coffee (or tea depending on whom I'm writing about) for the road. We were well fortified with food and drink when we left and arrived at the Santa Barbara Cathedral about fifteen minutes later. As we entered the docent asked us what language we spoke. She then handed us a flyer in English with all the stopping places numbered so we could read all about them.

There was a tour group of about twenty people directly ahead of us. Only the leader had the flyer, and when he wanted everyone to gather around to listen to his story he would raise his black, very official-looking umbrella like he was Mary Poppins in disguise.

That's exactly what Jean and I did. When I was about to read a section I raised my umbrella and Jean would rush back and gather around waiting for my pearls of wisdom. When I got tired of reading I gave her the flyer and the umbrella and she would do the honors. We spent more time laughing than actually reading. The tour guide ahead of us was not particularly impressed with our giggling but his evil eye and scrunched-up forehead did not seem to deter us.....just made us laugh longer and louder.

Czeching Out

In the rain Jean and I walked from one end of the town to the other. Most of the churches and interesting spots were closed but we did make it to The Church of All Saints with the Ossuary (memorial place for bones). The inside was decorated, and I use that term loosely, with bones and skulls and complete skeletons. There were piles and piles and piles of skulls in all the corners. Bones were made into chandeliers, tables, chalices, and the coat of arms of the house of Schwarzenberg. It was so strange, somewhat gruesome, but mostly just weird. It was definitely something we had never seen before, despite all our travels. Although the signs prohibiting it, and even though I had purchased many postcards of the interior, I took a few flash pictures.

We talked about our day on our walk back through the town. We took the train straight back to Prague without changing in Kolm. At the train station we bought some dinner to take home.....half a roasted chicken, a couple of salads, chips and some cookies. We picked up a bottle of wine before heading back to our room to soak our feet. We ate dinner in our room and, since it had been so different, rehashed our day, making sure that we remembered everything so I could update my notes. It had been most fascinating and enjoyable despite the fact that it had been long and dreary weather-wise.

We checked our funds. The travel agency had wanted one thousand four-hundred Kroner each for the tour to Kutna Hora. We had taken the same tour for just over two hundred Kroner and our tour had included breakfast in an adorable, little doll house.

It was a heck of a mark-up!

Chapter 11

The Old Jewish Quarter

It rained again on our last day in Prague but somehow it seemed fitting to be rainy and drab on this day. Today Jean, my friend and constant companion on this trip, and I visited the Old Jewish Quarter.

Our first stop was the Old-New Synagogue. This temple dates from the year twelve hundred seventy or possibly twelve hundred eighty AD. It stands on the original site and is Prague's oldest Gothic monument, and one of the oldest and best-preserved synagogues in Europe. The massive stone construction helped it survive in the face of fires, floods and other natural disasters. It survived the pogroms. It is still used for prayer services by the remaining Jewish community.

It was Yom Kippur (The Day of Atonement) and the synagogue would be closing at two in the afternoon. It was Sunday, the twenty-second of September in the year nineteen ninety-six. It had been our plan to go through the synagogue first because of its early closing. When I looked at my block of tickets I realized that each of the different museums had a time stamp on it and we must go through this portion first or we would not be admitted at all after the time expired.

We had waited in a long line, and once inside I was resentful of the extra money we paid to visit the Old-New Synagogue. They had charged everyone an additional eight American dollars, over and above the rest of the ticket. It was our last day and I felt that we could have used the money elsewhere since our funds were running very low. The temple was so small and barren that at first sight it didn't seem worth it.

Czeching Out

Before entering the main part of the temple we noticed a small enclosed blockhouse at the back and I asked another tourist if she knew what the house was used for. She opened a guidebook, found the proper page and explained that when additions or funding were needed for the synagogue the money was placed there for safekeeping.

"The Jews were also very heavily taxed," she explained still reading the guide, "and that money was kept there as well."

"Considering what it cost to get in here," I said, "we are still heavily taxed." Both she and Jean chuckled a little too loud and I hoped that no one else had overheard my insensitive remark.

Inside the house of worship, even with so many people around, Jean and I decided that we wanted to 'feel' the peace if there was any. We sat on the wooden benches that lined the sides of the synagogue and tried to meditate. We found that there were too many people milling around and when I couldn't concentrate, I poked her so she couldn't concentrate either. We sat in silence, and looked around the room, taking it all in: the speaker's tribune with the interior divided into two naves, political and religious. There was the red banner with the Star of David. There was the pointed hat that had been given to the community by Ferdinand I for helping to defend it against the Swedes in the year sixteen hundred and forty-eight AD. We spotted the slots in the windows for women to view the services but not to participate in them. And we watched all the people milling around, our favorite thing to do as we traveled the country.

From the Old-New Synagogue we went to the Maislova Synagogue. Mordecai Maisel purchased the land in the year fifteen ninety AD to build his own house of worship. In its time the Maislova Synagogue was the most revered shul (synagogue) in the community. Mr. & Mrs. Maisel donated many of the artifacts housed there. Like many other synagogues it was destroyed by fire and rebuilt more simply in sixteen ninety-one. The temple's originator did not live to see the new place of worship. He died in sixteen hundred and one AD.

From Maislova we walked around the corner to the Pinkas Synagogue, dedicated to the people of Czechoslovakia who died in the holocaust. The temple was devoid of artifacts and painted pure white, a symbol of mourning. Any words spoken within those walls were done so in whispers.

The name of each victim was inscribed on the walls. Seventy-seven thousand, two hundred and ninety-seven names, all printed perfectly. The family name was printed only once and the given names and dates followed. Wall after wall after wall. Name after name after name. Every letter was perfectly formed – the names, the dates they were born and the dates of their deportation to the death camp. A little plaque, hanging on a rope standing two feet away from the wall, signified what city, town or village the victims came from. Their entire existence was printed in one small space on a wall. The experience was numbing.

While Jean shook her head and commented, over and over, whispering the birth dates of the children, my eyes went from name to name looking for mine, even with a variation in spelling. Only one name came close, but my family background is Rumanian not Czechoslovakian.

The second floor was the same as the first. The third floor was the same as the first and second but everyone there was compelled to go on. We went.....even if it was just to say, "we know that you lived." We were simply paying our respects.

My flippancy from earlier in the day was gone. Jean and I walked the marble floor slowly and mostly in silence.

Czeching Out

Tears filled our eyes. There were so many names listed on those walls. So many people.....

For a few moments in the courtyard we talked softly and shared our feelings. I was not prepared for the horror or the emptiness that I felt.

From the Pinkas Synagogue we walked around the corner to the Old Jewish Cemetery. The original gravestones dated back to the thirteenth century while the last grave was dug in the year seventeen eighty-seven. There seemed to be no order. It was one of the most unusual and macabre cemeteries I had ever seen. A surreal configuration of leaning, fallen and crammed-together gravestones combined to total twelve thousand stones above ground with up to sixty thousand graves, in as many as twelve layers, below ground. Some headstones were in urgent need of repair while others stood erect, visible and prominent.

Jean and I found the tombs of Maisel, the principle figure in building and renovating Jewish buildings and homes during the renaissance, and Rabbi Löw, the most learned Talmudic scholar in Jewish history.

There were many tourists milling around, and since some people were whispering about the pebbles, I took the time to explain why they had been placed on top of the headstones.

"It is simply a sign of respect and remembrance," I explained. "Even when I visit the graves of my mother and father in a cemetery in Montreal, Canada I place a little pebble on their gravestone just to say I was there."

Several people in the group, including Jean and myself, picked up a few small stones and placed them on the markers.

After leaving the cemetery we entered the adjacent building. It was the Jewish Museum building and the home of pictures. The pictures came from Terezin about an hour's drive north of Prague. Terezin was Hitler's model city. The Jews were evacuated from Prague and placed in a ghetto there. They lived, worked, studied, painted, wrote and attended school there. This was where the rest of the world viewed its citizens. Once seen, they were sent to other concentration camps or executed at Terezin.

All the paintings, drawings, stories, poems and memorabilia were saved. Some paintings, bold and complex, were by adult artists. Some, simple and naïve, were drawn by Jewish children. The Old Jewish Quarter in Prague is the best preserved in the world. Hitler wanted it that way. This was to be "The Museum of an Extinct People."

Somehow it seemed fitting that it was raining in Prague on our last day. That evening Jean and I attended Yom Kippur services at the Spanish Temple in Prague.

The rain stopped!

Chapter 12

Departure Day

D-Day.....departure day!

We were not sorry to be leaving. The weather had been just too nasty more days than not, with Jack Frost nipping at our noses and an icy rain that cut through us like a machete through butter.

Despite the weather it had been an exciting journey, filled with unexpected pleasures and only a few disappointments, like not finding Franz Kafka's grave. Many of the sights had been incredible. The city of Prague is known for its hundred spires. We had not seen all of them but certainly enough to make us want to come back at another time, hopefully earlier in the year.

On that last morning we had been permitted to leave the luggage in our room until early afternoon, for which we were very grateful. I exchanged one of my few remaining U.S. twenty-dollar bills so we could have lunch and buy a few trinkets if we wanted to. We both were hungry, and we looked at each other before we started to laugh. Without saying a word we went straight towards our favorite pub, Pivniche, like we were being reeled in on a hook and line. A spicy meatball lunch with a basket full of sliced crusty bread to soak up the thick tomato-red sauce, the special of the day, was just what we needed to stave off starvation. We ate and drank for a couple of hours before sauntering through the Town Square one last time, and then back to the room to collect our things.

We took the subway to the train station. While it was still relatively warm and sunny outside we waited and waited and waited, both of us sitting on our luggage just outside the

Chasing the Lost Dream

main entrance. We just needed a place to sit since we didn't want to wander around dragging a back-breaking load of dirty laundry, and the train station was as good a place as any.

Just as we were about to leave and set off for another long wait at the bus depot an inspector stopped us for the first time since our arrival in the Czech Republic. He wanted to see our train tickets. Very tricky, these inspectors. He could have asked for our tickets at any time but waited until we had been there a couple of hours and were ready to board. Had we not purchased the tickets the fine would have been a lot more money than either of us had on hand. Fortunately, we had them. We left for the bus depot when we got tired of sitting and watching the same unattractive and boring scenery.

We arrived at our bus station three hours before departure time. While Jean sat with our luggage I went wandering. I discovered we were right across the street from a cemetery that had just locked its gates; I went to investigate. The sign on a pole right behind the locked gate in front of the main entrance said "Franz Kafka Grave" in big, black, bold lettering with an arrow pointing right. No wonder we couldn't find the grave - it was right in front of our noses when we arrived! And right in front of our noses when we left too! I could almost see Franz Kafka sticking his tongue out at me going "nah, nah, nah!" The cemetery had closed early because of Yom Kippur.

The Scandia Bus out of Prague was far more comfortable than our prisoner-of-war reject (due to inhuman treatment) bus on the way to Prague. We hadn't progressed very far when our bus made an unexpected and unscheduled stop beside a large field. An elderly couple, in their late sixties or possibly seventies, got on. Their luggage was put in the baggage compartment and they found seats near ours. We really thought they were dignitaries until we started talking to

238

them. It seems that their landlady in Prague had taken them to the Florence Station instead of Zivnehs Station, and while they were racing to the Florence Station they saw their bus go by. They chased it, flagged it down and got on board in the middle of nowhere. Not exactly in "dignitary" style but they were delighted to be on board and heading home.

The movie playing on the bus was *Field of Dreams* with Kevin Costner, in Czech, of course. We left in the rain and the rain followed us most of the way.

The bus was packed! I slept little!

Chapter 13

Homeward Bound

If it's Tuesday it must be Belgium. It was Tuesday and we were in Belgium. Many of our fellow travelers had gotten off in Brussels and almost no one had gotten on so we had room to spread out. It suddenly felt like everyone could undo their belts and Jean and I laughed at the uniformed sigh of relief.

The return trip had been reasonably comfortable and uneventful.....for us anyway. Every time we crossed one of the several borders our passports were taken from us by an official-looking officer in uniform, and a few minutes later some poor guy, sitting just across and one seat down from me, was escorted off the bus. I didn't particularly like his appearance but couldn't figure out why he was always singled out for special attention.

"Christ," he said really loudly when he returned. "I'm getting sick and tired of being strip-searched at every crossing."

"Can I have a look at your passport?" I asked, my curiosity getting the better of me. "May I make a suggestion?" I said, after looking at his picture.

"Sure," he replied with a bit of a sneer.

"Cut your hair, shave, remove your nose ring, cover up the tattoos on your neck and for Christ' sake get a new passport picture."

He laughed. "Maybe you're right," he said in a typical British accent, and to which I replied, "unless, of course, you're starting to enjoy the stripping and the searching." We both laughed out loud and I couldn't believe how cute he was under all that hair. He became very chatty and we had a long conversation about where we were from, where we had been

Czeching Out

and how long we had been away. He was fascinated by my years of wanderlust.

Without the rain the scenery was a little more interesting. Jean and I each had a bowl of beef and vegetable soup and half a sandwich on the Pride of Burgundy Ferry as we crossed over the channel into England.

The bus from Victoria Station in London to Bristol was comfortable and fast, but we were really tired and Bill, Jean's husband, looked like a knight in shining armor as he waited at the station to greet us. You could see in his eyes how thrilled he was to have Jean home, and he let us chatter on like magpies on the twelve-mile trip to Temple Cloud. Dinner was held for us and put on the table, piping hot, the minute we walked through the door.

I took a long, soothing bath. We relaxed on the couch. "Laying DOWN to take a nap – what a novel idea," I said, having just spent several days sleeping upright. That was the last thing I remember. I fell asleep in less than thirty seconds.

We had only been gone fourteen days.....it sure felt longer than that!

Epilogue

Chasing the Lost Dream

In the end I found what I was searching for: a strength within me that lay dormant during the years that I was a happily married woman. It was that strength that helped me to decide that I would give myself the best possible life without hoping for someone to come along and 'rescue me.' If I chose I could continue to travel and make worldwide friends, like I had done in the past, or I could sit contentedly and read or write.

I gave myself permission to grieve for my Paul anywhere in the world I happen to be, in any way I felt like it, and for as long as I chose. He was my soul mate and I miss him with a piece of my heart that I have reserved only for him.

I also found the strength to tell others, perhaps not quite so brave, my story.

I will continue chasing my dreams, but more importantly I will create new ones.

About the Author:

Joei Carlton Hossack was born in February of 1944 and raised in Montreal, Quebec, Canada. She has lived in Toronto, Canada, Los Angeles, California and Sarasota, Florida. She spent most of the last seventeen years traveling the world in various recreational vehicles and now makes her winter home in Surrey, British Columbia. She spends her summers traveling, gathering stories and lecturing.

She is the author of six adventure travel books, a member of the B.C. Association of Travel Writers and an entertaining speaker specializing in world travel, full-time RVing and writing/publishing/promotion.

Joei can be reached at: JoeiCarlton@Hotmail.com
                            SkeenaPress@Hotmail.com

Website: www.joeicarlton.com